The Batsford
ENCYCLOPAEDIA OF
EMBROIDERY STITCHES

The Batsford ENCYCLOPAEDIA OF EMBROIDERY STITCHES

Anne Butler

photographs by John Hunnex

B T Batsford Limited *London*

First published 1979
Revised edition 1982
First published in paperback 1983
ISBN 0 7134 3849 5

Printed and bound in Great Britain by
Anchor Brendon Ltd, Tiptree, Essex
for the Publishers B T Batsford Limited,
4 Fitzhardinge Street London W1H 0AH

CONTENTS

INTRODUCTION

When using the stitch diagrams in this book please take particular note of the following points.

1 In order to make the process of producing the stitch as clear as possible, the length of both the thread and the needle varies from diagram to diagram. The reader should therefore ignore the lengths of needle or thread and not attempt to relate them to other diagrams or to his or her own needle and thread.

2 The needle is always shown as going in and out of the fabric except when the diagram is marked ntf (not through the fabric). In these instances the needle is usually going under a thread which is already a part of the stitch being made.

3 Many of the stitches have more than one name — sometimes six or even more. I have chosen what I consider to be the most common or appropriate name in an attempt to make the book more easily useable though I realise that my own choice will obviously not be that of everyone. It could be that the names used here may form the basis of a standard reference. The stitches are grouped in families to assist the reader in identification and selection.

Historically, the relative cost of embroidery threads has often dictated the type of stitch used. Wool has traditionally been plentiful and cheap, whilst silk has, in different periods been either cheap or expensive. Metal threads have always been relatively expensive.

If an embroiderer chooses to cover all the background fabric then large quantities of thread may be used up and an inexpensive background fabric chosen to balance this cost. Shorter lengths of thread are used if a speckle stitch or thin line stitch is selected. Braid and chain stitches waste only a little thread on the back of the fabric and couched stitches can incorporate a cheaper thread used to hold down the main thread. In many historical periods the choice of stitches used has been influenced by such economic and practical considerations as much as a desire for the perfect visual effect.

The contemporary embroiderer, with a great number of stitches from which to choose, should choose the stitches primarily for the quality of effect which they produce. This may be to produce a line, filling, a directional quality or surface texture.

The degree of complexity of the diagrams in this book bear no relationship to the degree of difficulty or ease of making. Some apparently simple stitches are quite difficult to master, whereas many simply worked stitches may appear complicated when seen in diagrammatic form. Some stitches will perhaps be more effective worked in a fine thread, some rely on the use of a coarse thread, whilst many are capable of production in a wide range of thread thicknesses.

The visual effect of most stitches is controlled by the thickness of the thread used, and other differences will occur when working the stitches in either a regular or irregular way. It should be noted that the majority of the stitches illustrated in this book have been worked in Atlas 36 macramé thread on a hessian fabric to provide a degree of uniformity of illustration throughout the book. A few examples have been worked in a finer thread on other background fabrics to overcome the problem of scale. Some stitches are best worked in a frame, these are usually examples where the first stage is loose and is subsequently held down by a second stage of stitches worked on top. One example of this is couching. In general it is best to work the stitches in the hand, this not only being easier to handle but usually giving a better visual effect.

The difficulty of working some stitches, and the inappropriate choice of thread or fabric may result in the background fabric being puckered. If this should occur it is important that the embroidery is stretched and not ironed. The puckering can be removed by this method and the surface and the thread will not be damaged.

Stitches are produced by the needle and the thread being inserted and brought out of the fabric at specific intervals. This action, the repitition of actions, and grouping of threads, can produce an endless variety of surfaces and combinations of effects. Many stitches are made up of a combination of other stitches and it is difficult to define what is a variation of a stitch, or a stitch in its own right.

Just how difficult can be seen from the following exercise. To make a line of stitches on a piece of fabric, work the stitches towards you. Start with a chain stitch (a), make a single feather stitch (b), then a buttonhole stitch (c), take the buttonhole stitch from side to side and you have cretan stitch (d), change again one position of the needle and make a herringbone stitch (e). Each stitch is developed from the other by merely altering the position of the needle.

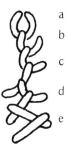

a
b
c
d
e

Some of the best descriptive writing of stitches is in *Modern Design in Embroidery* by Rebecca Crompton published by Batsford. Although this book is out of print it is worth trying to buy a copy from a second hand book shop or to borrow one from a library. It contains the following passages: 'the stitch has an irregular surface, the effect of which breaks up the light'; 'surface darning suggests a woven texture and can be subjected to all sorts of variation in relation to the arrangement of colour in the warp and weft effect'; 'some are smooth in their general effect, some give a knotty surface, some have definite direction, whilst others spread out equally in all directions'.

Anne Butler
Stockport 1979

UNRELATED LINE STITCHES

Double knot stitch

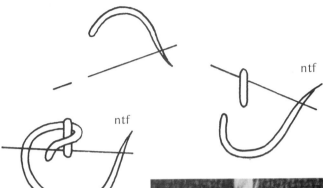

Split stitch

Needle comes up here
and splits thread

Bell stitch

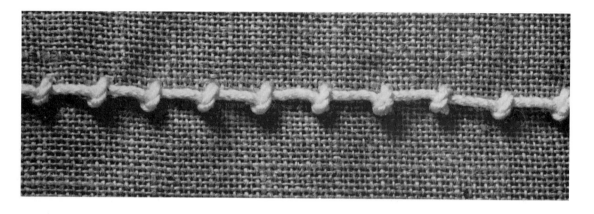

Pearl stitch

Pull the needle down
through the loop

 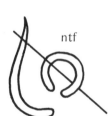 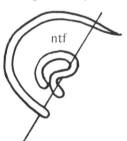 

ntf

ntf

Knot stitch

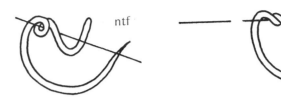

Twist the thread
round needle twice

Wick stitch

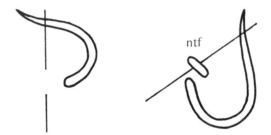

Scroll stitch

Roll stitch

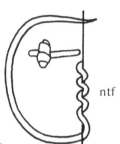
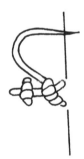

ntf

The thread is twisted
around the needle and
then needle drawn through

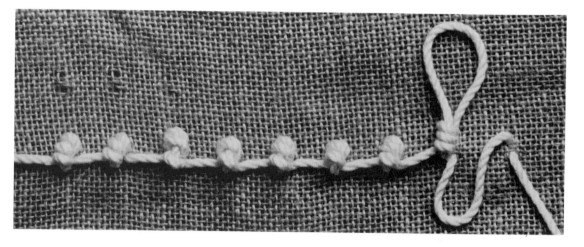

Knotted pearl stitch

Continue stage 3, stage 4, 3, 4 and so on

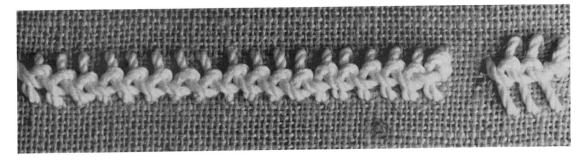

Breton stitch

  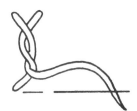

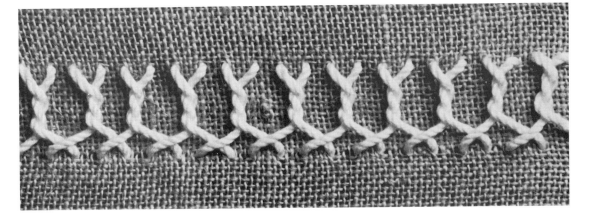

Laced knot stitch

Well stitch

Knotted diamond stitch

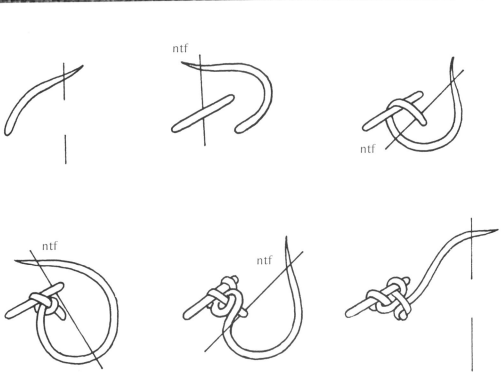

Plaited braid stitch

 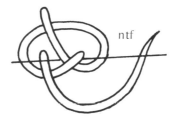 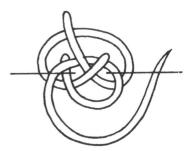

Work the first stage once only and repeat
second and third stages

Complete repeat of the separate unit

'Sham' hem zigzag stitch

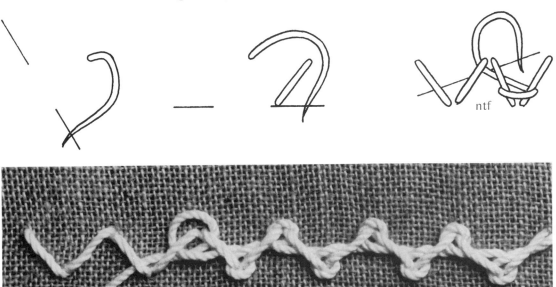

Wing stitch

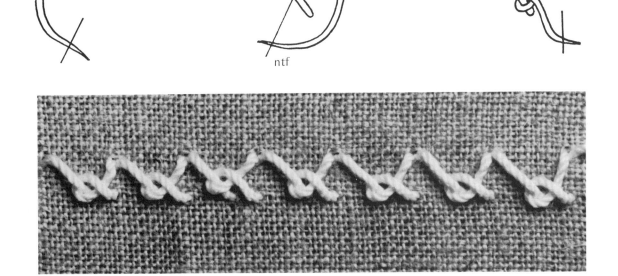

Ladder stitch

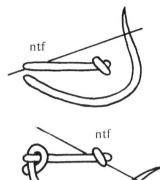

ntf

ntf

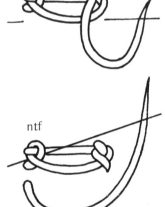

ntf

Wheatear stitch

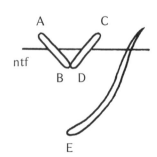

A   C

ntf

B D

E

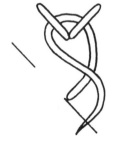

Sheaf stitch

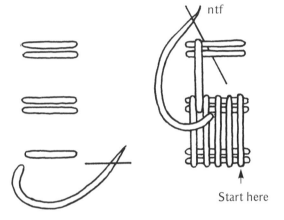

ntf

Start here

ntf

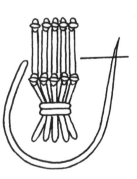

The stitches are worked
across interlocked area

COUCHINGS

Underside couching

Thread up and down same hole
NB Couched so thread is pulled through fabric, back is as shown in B, top in A

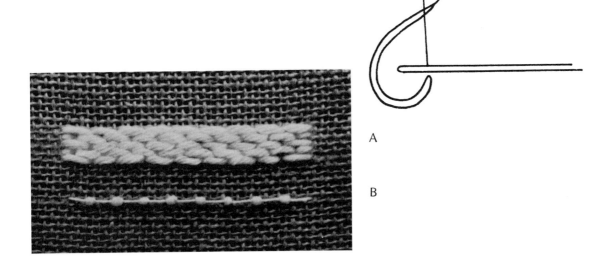

A

B

Couching

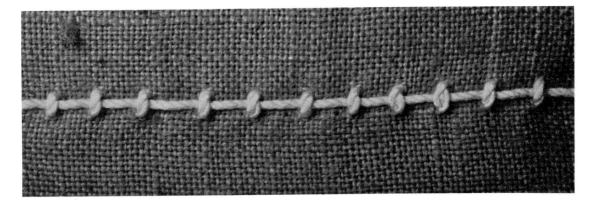

Various couchings (1)

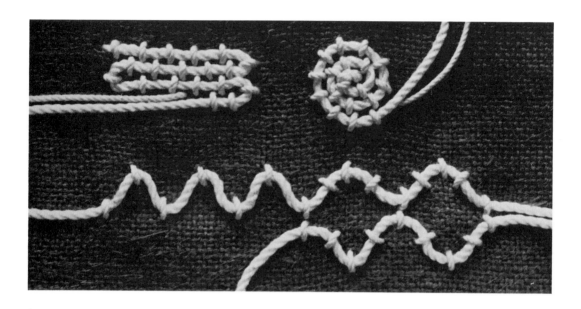

Various couchings (2)

Puffy couching

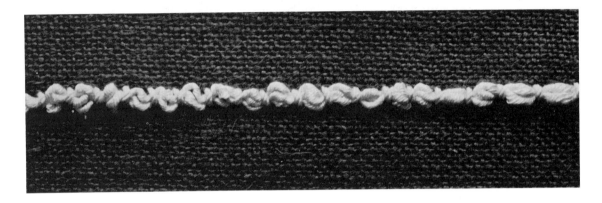

Pendant couching

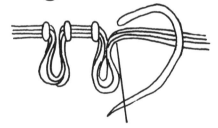

Thorn stitch

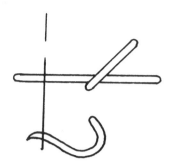

Steps and diagonal stitch

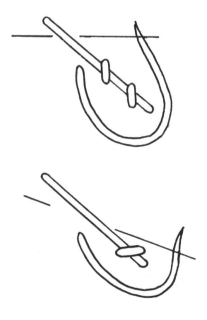

Trailing stitch

Overcast stitch

Over a running stitch

Satin stitch braid-like border
and Persian border couching stitch

Persian border couching   Satin stitch braid-like border

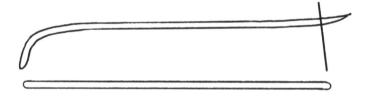

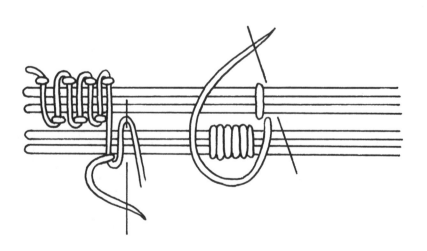

Couching raised band and plate

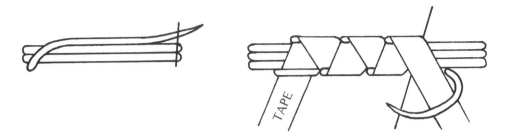

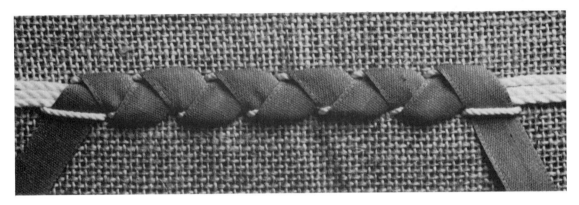

Bokhara couching

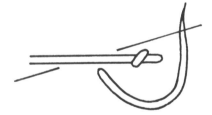

Laid base

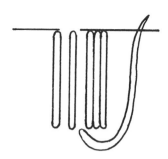

Laid work stitches

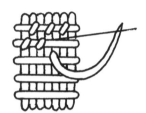

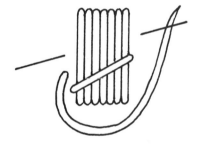
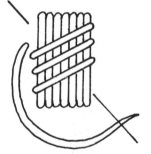
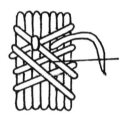

Tied diagonally laid work

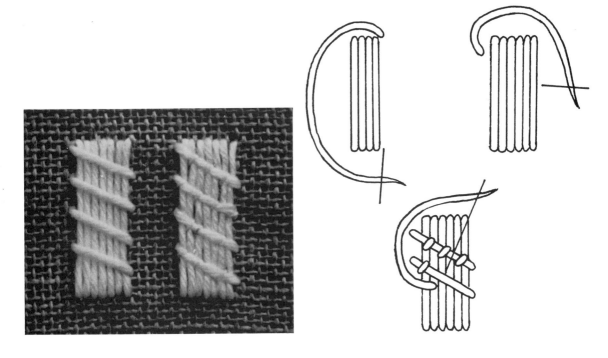

Solid laid work

Curved lines in any pattern

New England laid stitch

Roumanian stitch

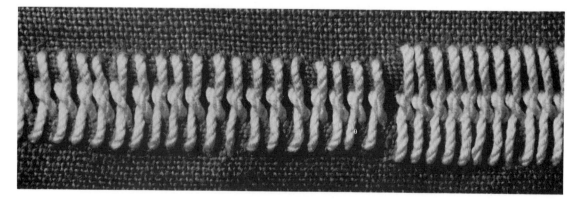

Roman stitch
and Roman filling stitch

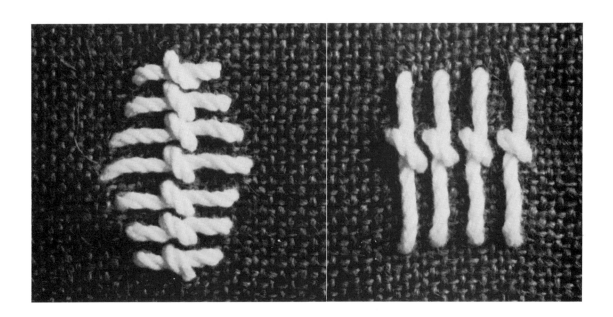

Roumanian couching

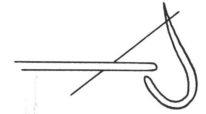

STEM STITCHES

Stem stitch (1)

Stem stitch (2)

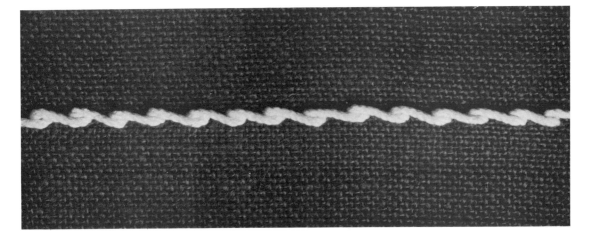

Filling stem stitch

Whipped stem stitch

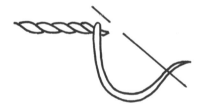 

ntf

Threaded stem stitch

First two rows of stem stitch

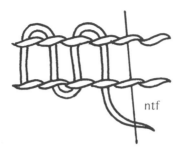

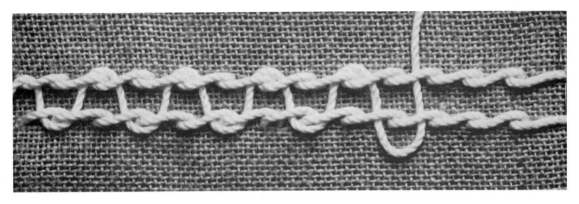

Side stem stitch

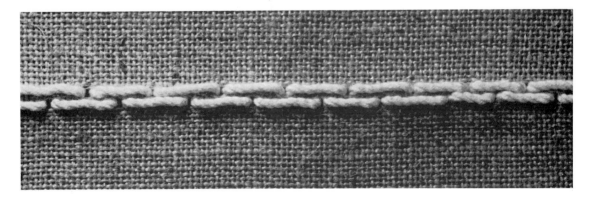

Reversed stem stitch

Outline stitch

Detached overcast stitch

Double stem stitch

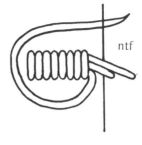

ntf

Overcast stitch

Encroaching satin stitch

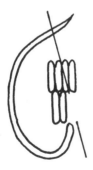

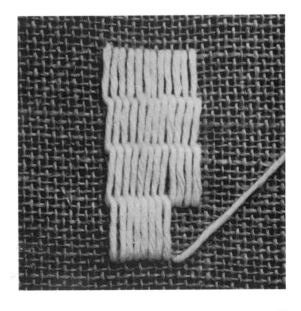

Plate stitch

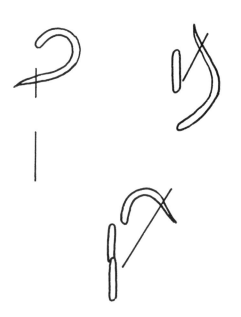

Double flast stitch

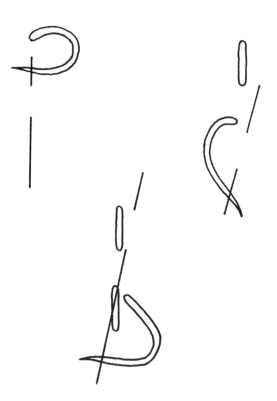

Portuguese stem stitch

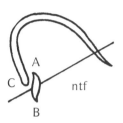

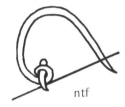

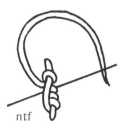

Whipped broad stem stitch

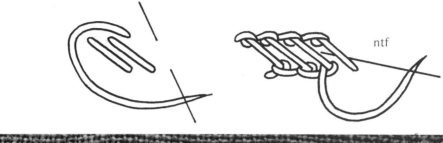

Looped stem stitch

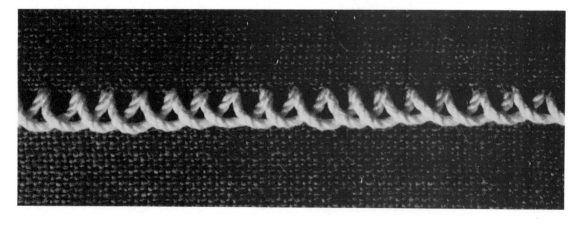

Fancy hem stitch

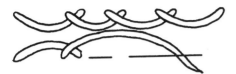
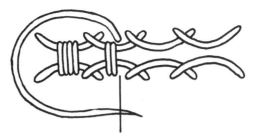

Chevron stem stitch

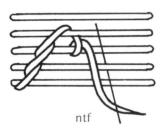

ntf

Portuguese border stitch

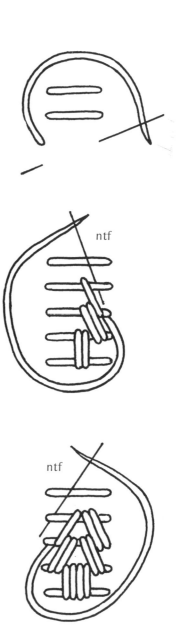

Lock stitch

ntf

ntf

Raised band stem stitch

ntf

ntf

Band raised stem stitch

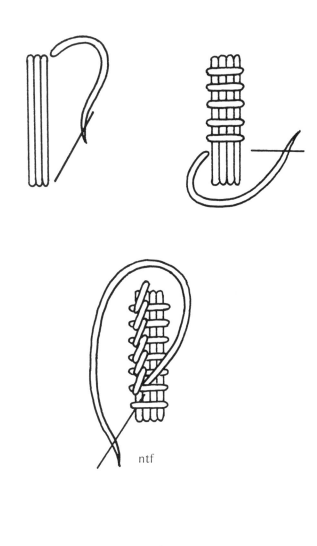

ntf

RUNNING AND BACK STITCHES

Line double running stitch
and area double running stitch

The stitch finished — single line

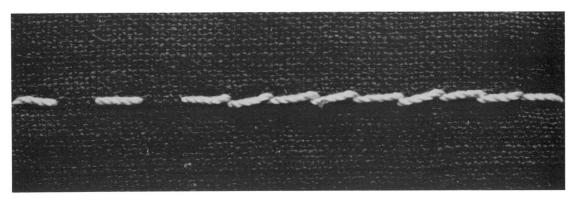

Several lines together

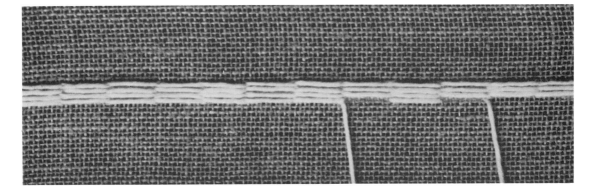

Long and short stitch

Dot stitch

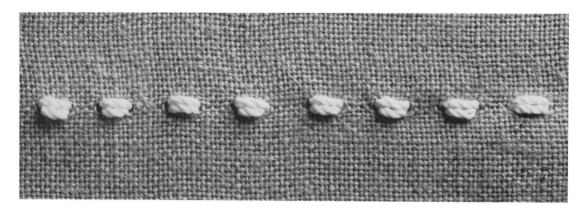

Treble running stitch

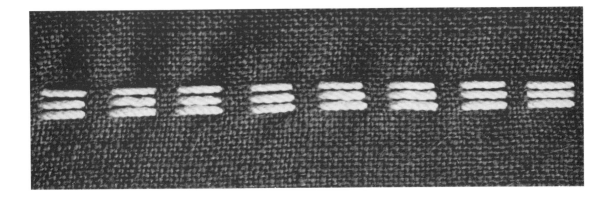

Dog-tooth edge

Burden stitch
and darning stitch

The length of stitch and gap between stitches is important

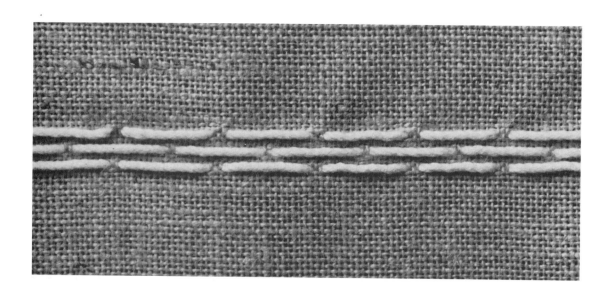

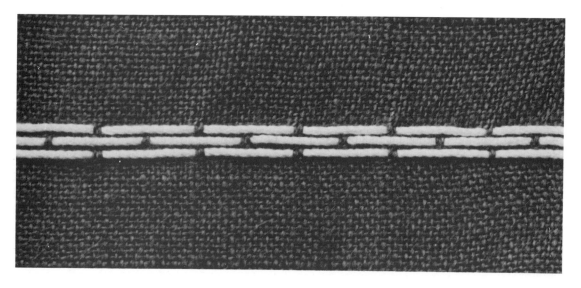

Battlement line stitch

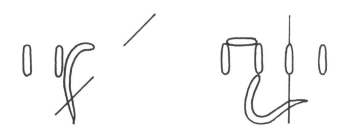

Eskimo lacing stitch

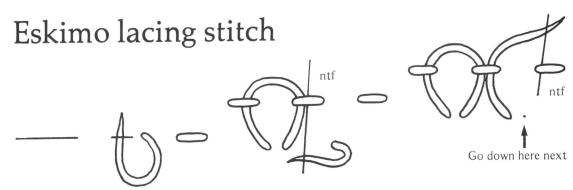

ntf

ntf

Go down here next

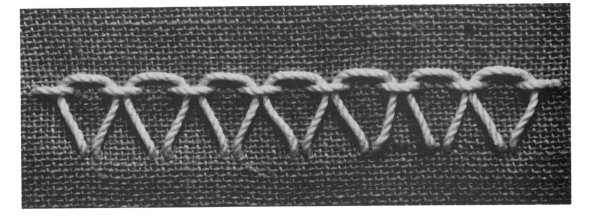

Double running steps

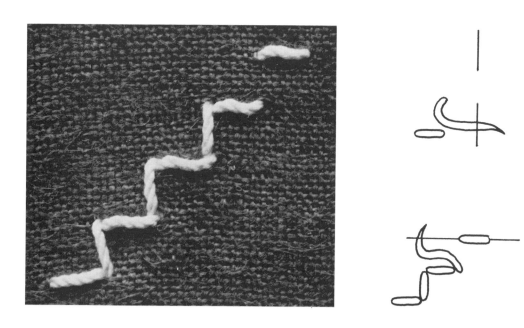

Double running stitch

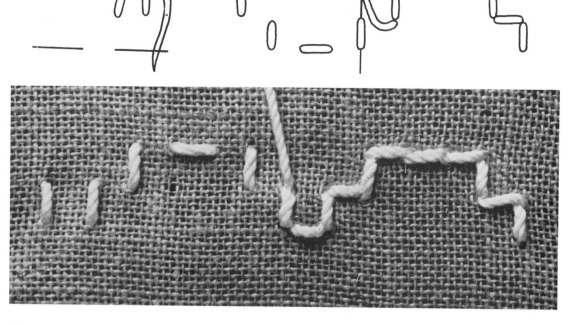

Candlewicking

Rows of running stitch are cut to achieve this

 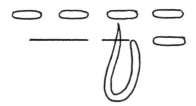

Interlaced running stitch

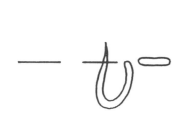 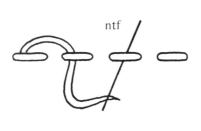 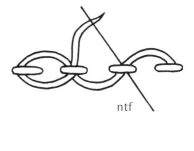

Interlaced double running stitch

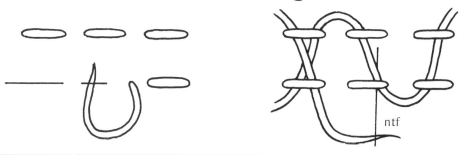

Laced double running stitch

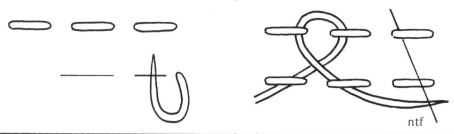

Laced stepped double stitch

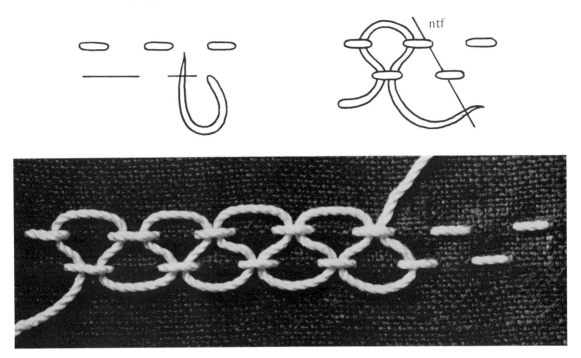

Threaded running stitch

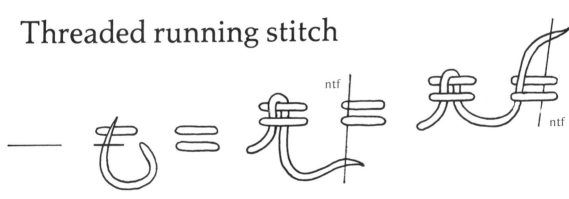

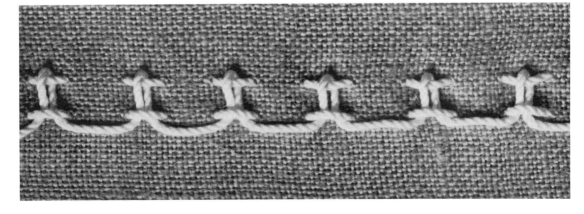

Double laced running stitch and double pekinese stitch

Double Pekinese stitch

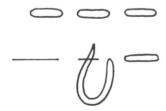

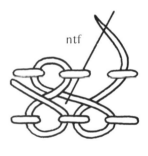

ntf

Laced double running stitch

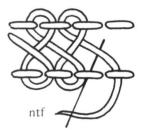

ntf

Laced treble running stitch

If this is threaded through again it becomes threaded treble running stitch

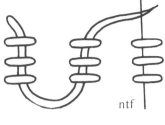

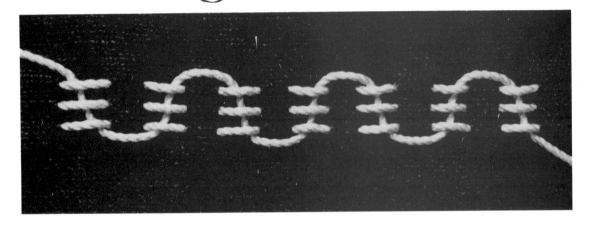

Threaded treble running stitch

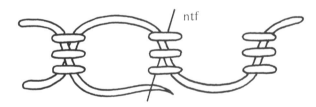

Laced running stitch
and whipped running stitch

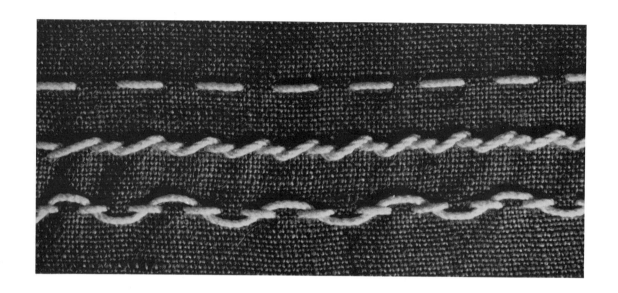

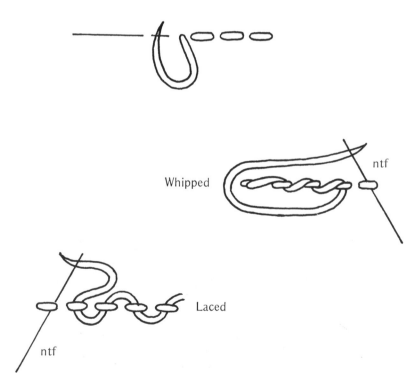

Whipped

ntf

Laced

ntf

Back stitch

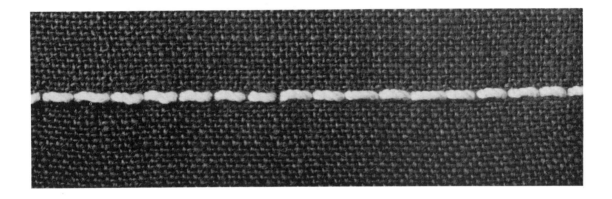

Threaded back stitch

ntf

Can be left at this stage as a single stitch

ntf

Pekinese stitch

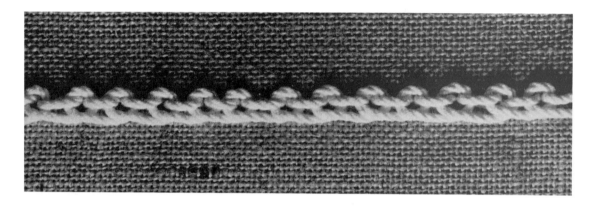

Trellis back stitch

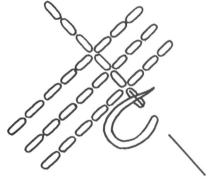

Festoon stitch

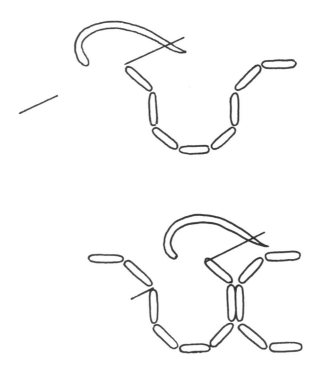

HERRINGBONE STITCHES

Herringbone stitch

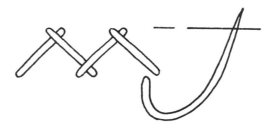

Double back stitch

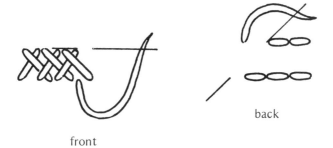

front

back

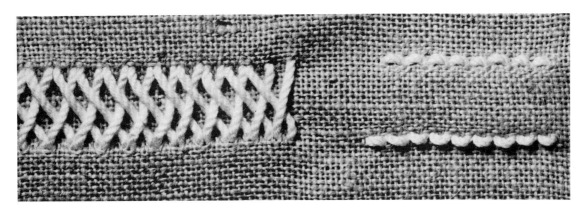

Double Herringbone stitch

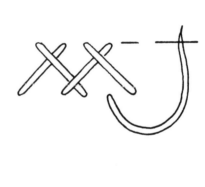

Criss cross herringbone stitch

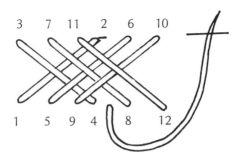

Plaited herringbone stitch

Square herringbone stitch

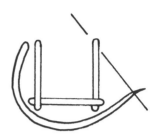

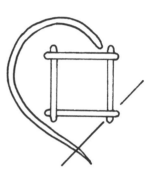

Raised close herringbone stitch

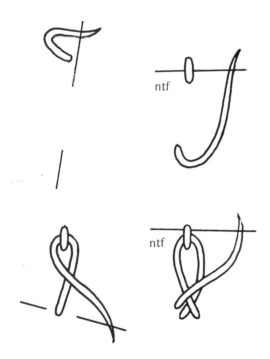

Back stitched herringbone stitch

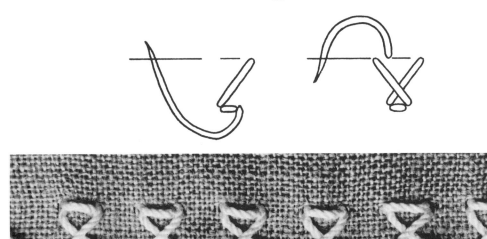

Threaded herringbone stitch

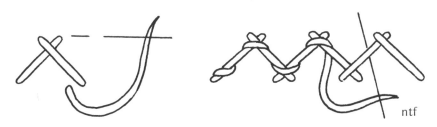

ntf

Herringbone and spike stitch

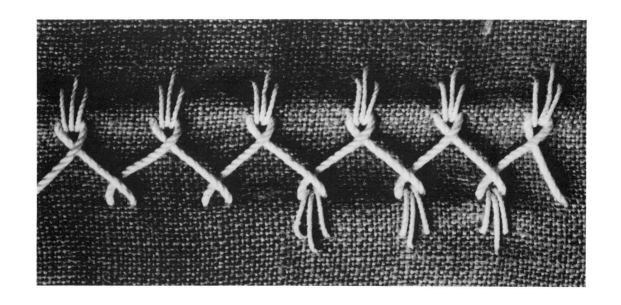

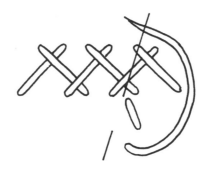

Tied herringbone stitch

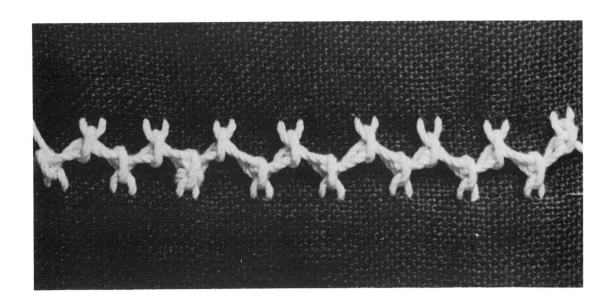

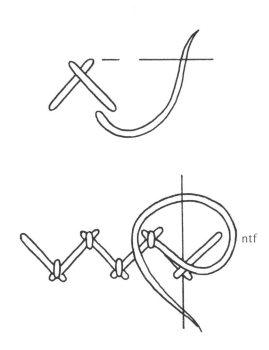

ntf

Twisted lattice band stitch

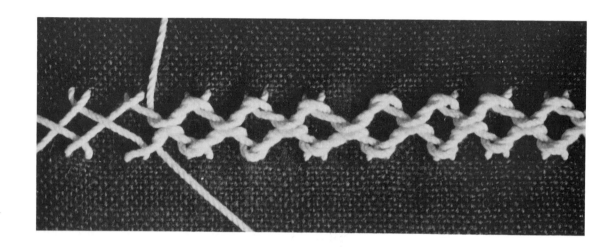

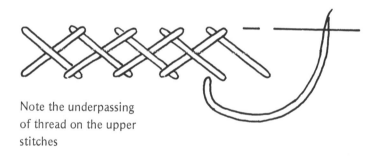

Note the underpassing
of thread on the upper
stitches

ntf

Point de reprise stitch

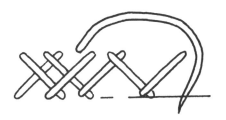

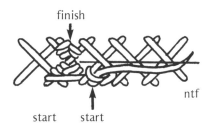

Start each one separately
Like needleweaving from outside
edge as far as centre crossing

Buttonholed herringbone stitch

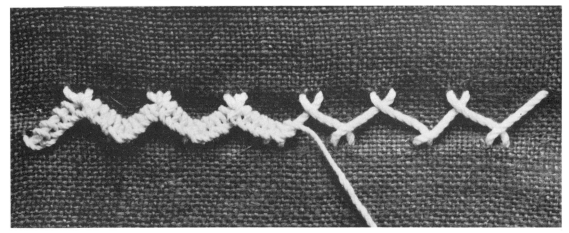

Laced herringbone stitch

Needle under thread, not over

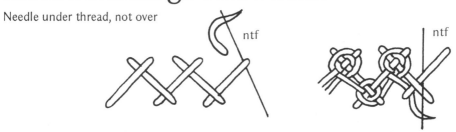

Fancy herringbone stitch

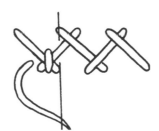
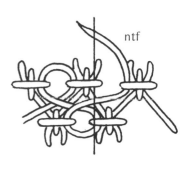

Interlaced herringbone stitch

Note the underpassing of thread on the upper stitches and on the centre upward direction stitches
Note two rows of herringbone stitch worked in a different way

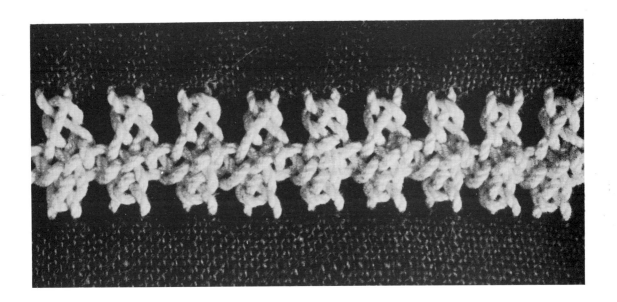

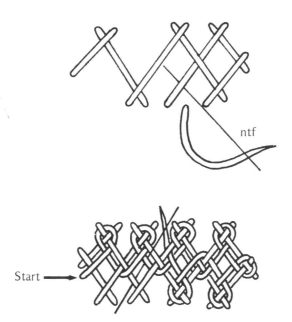

ntf

Start ⟶

Raised laced band stitch

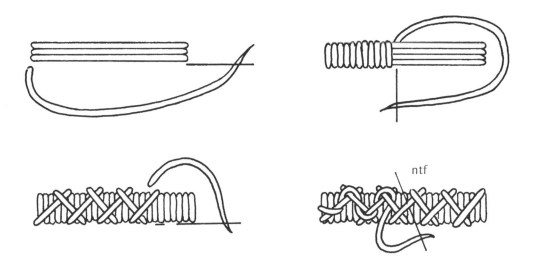

Fancy herringbone stitch

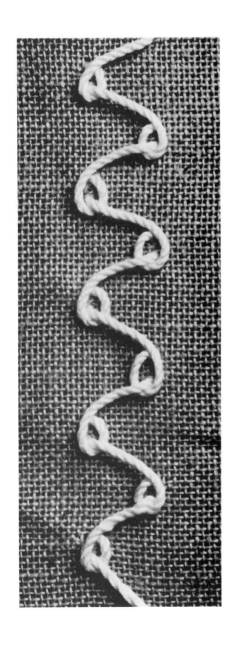

FEATHER STITCHES

Single feather stitch

Feather stitch

Laced feather stitch

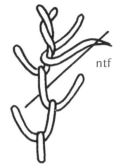

ntf

Knotted feather stitch

ntf

Double feather stitch

Double and treble feather stitch

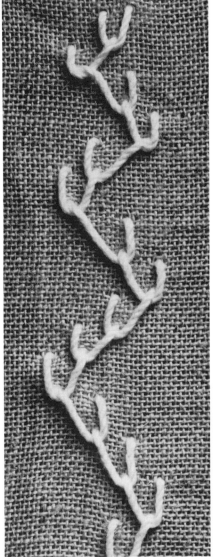

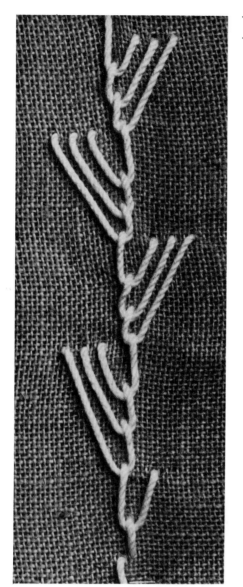

Maidenhair stitch

Double chain stitch

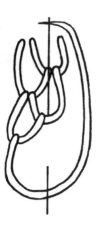

Closed feather stitch

Inverted feather stitch

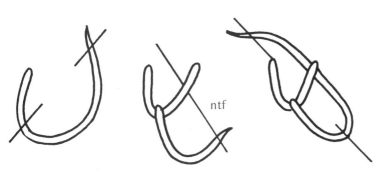

ntf

Spanish knotted feather stitch

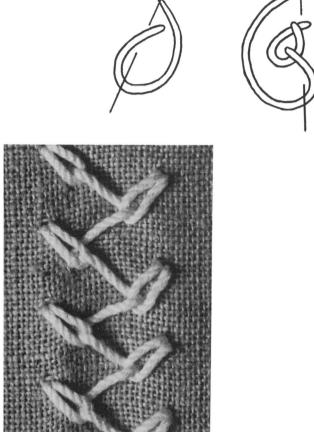

Chained feather stitch

Thorn stitch

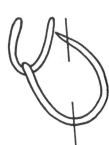

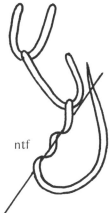

ntf

Twist thread
around needle

Floral feather stitch

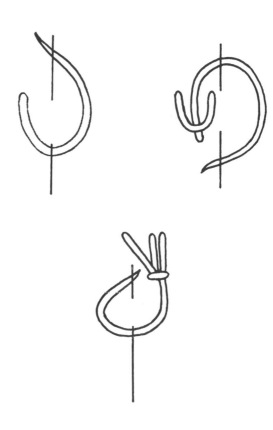

Leaf filling stitch

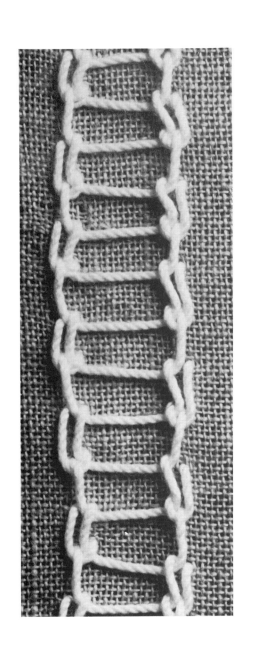

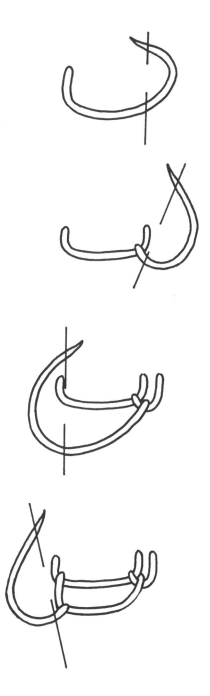

Raised band feather stitch

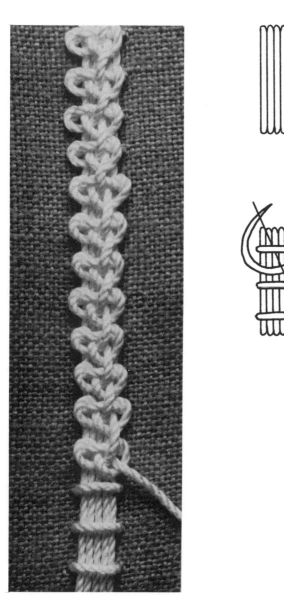

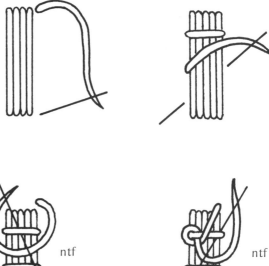

ntf

ntf

FLY STITCHES

Single fly stitch

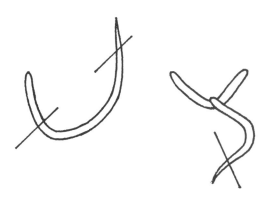

Use of fly stitch

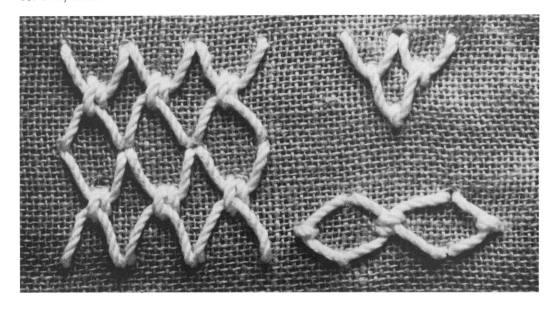

Attached fly stitch
and whipped fly stitch

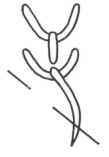

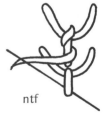

ntf

Flowing fly stitch

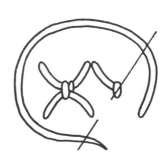

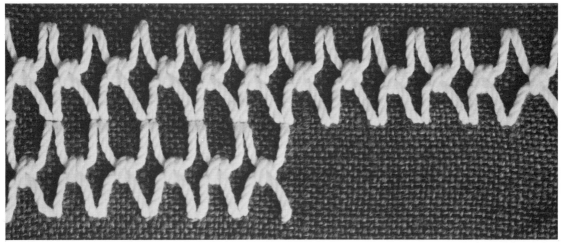

Plaited fly stitch

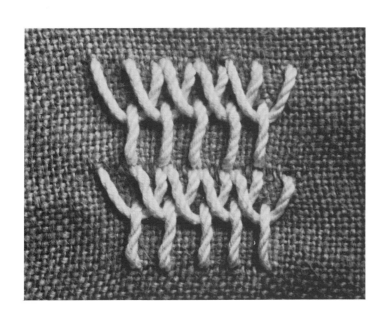

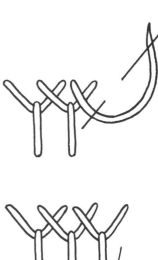

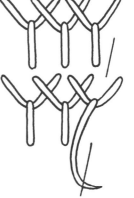

Double fly stitch

Reversed fly stitch

Closed fly stitch

Interlaced fly stitch

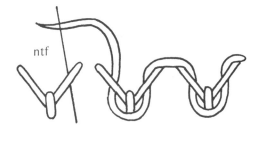

ntf

CRETAN STITCHES

Slipped cretan and half cretan

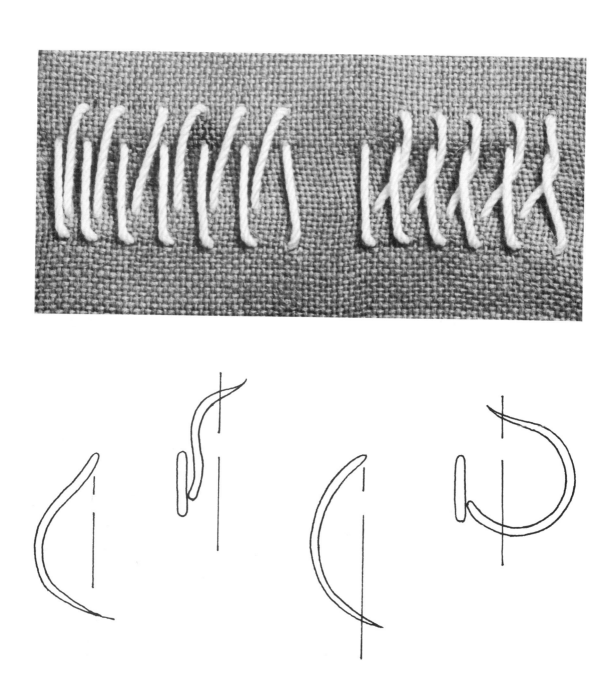

Cretan stitch

The effect can be varied by the closeness and length of stitch

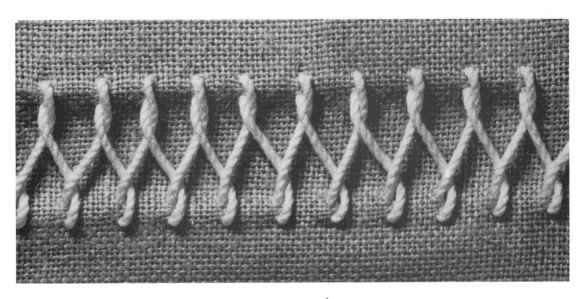

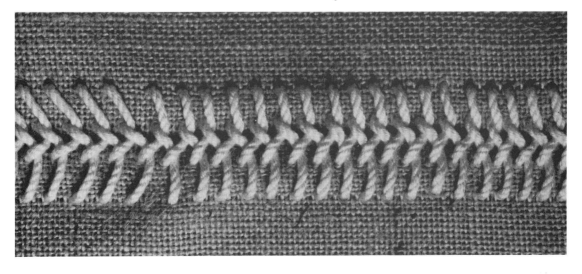

A use of cretan stitch

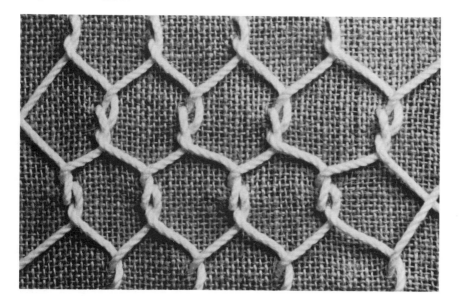

Knotted cretan stitch

Oriental stitch

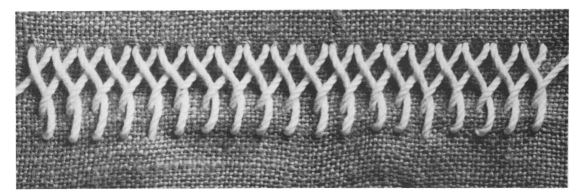

Scotch cretan stitch

Cretan stitch is worked in groups and then threaded as shown

ntf

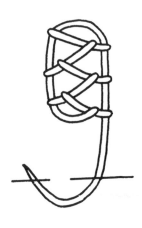

Crossed cretan stitch

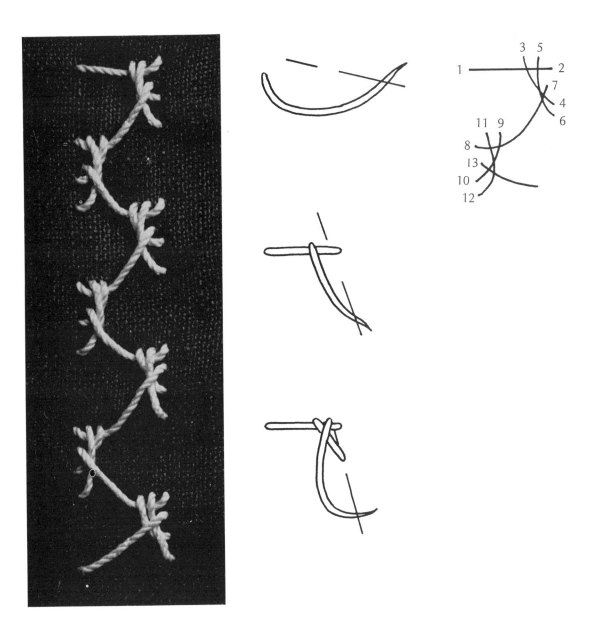

Looped cretan stitch

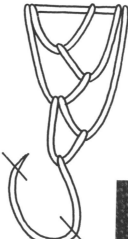

Tied cretan stitch

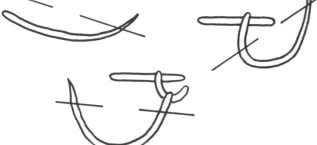

French cretan stitch

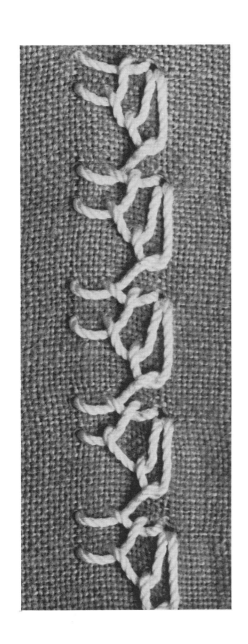

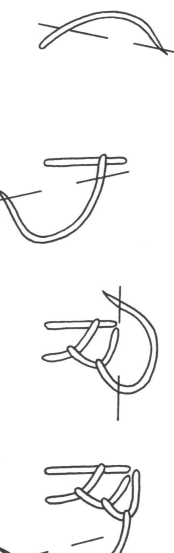

Raised cretan stitch

 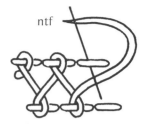

Cretan open filling stitch

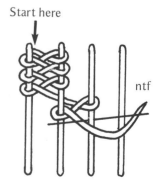

120

BUTTONHOLE
STITCHES

Various buttonhole stitches

Blanket stitch

Buttonhole stitch is the same but the stitches are
worked closer together

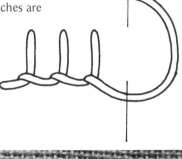

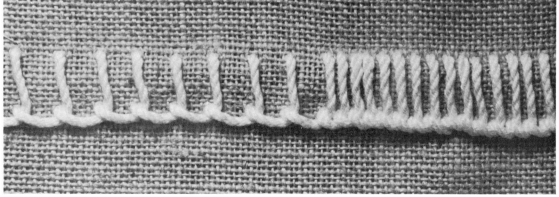

Closed buttonhole stitch

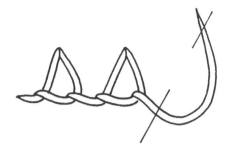

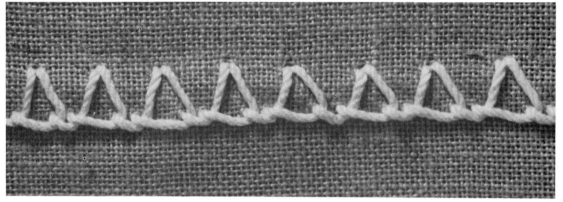

Crossed buttonhole stitch

Triangular formation buttonhole stitch

Rosette of thorns stitch

Up and down buttonhole stitch

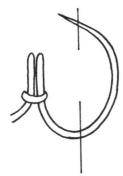 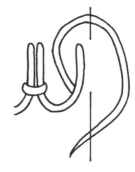

Tailor's buttonhole stitch

The thread is twisted around the needle

Tailor's buttonhole stitch with picot

The thread is twisted around the needle

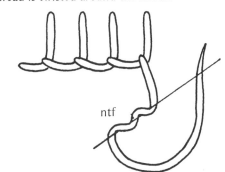

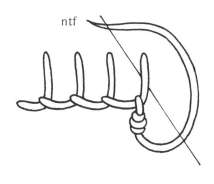

Knotted buttonhole

Twist thread around the needle

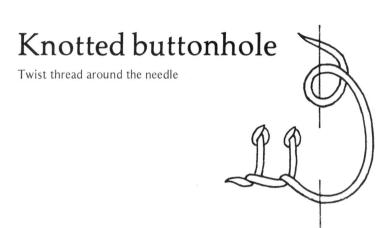

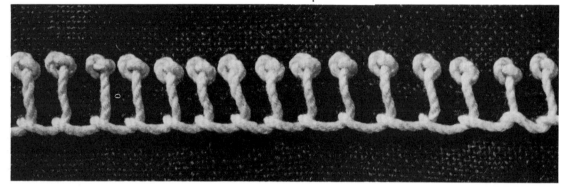

Pulled buttonhole stitch

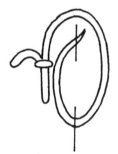

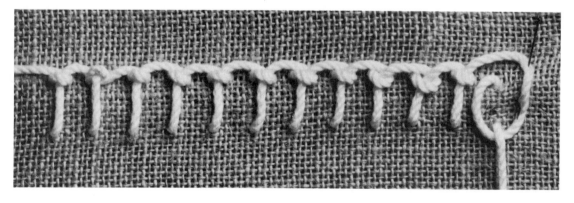

Looped edge stitch

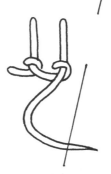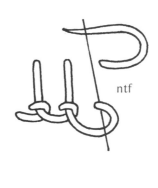

ntf

Berwick stitch

Thread twisted
around needle

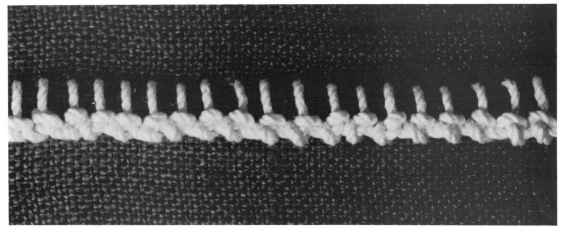

Tailor's buttonhole and stem stitch

Whipped buttonhole stitch

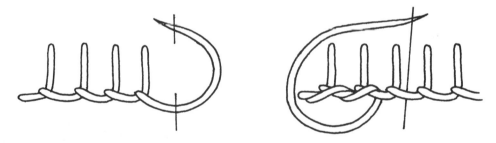

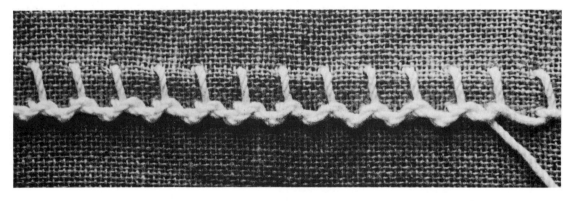

Single coral stitch

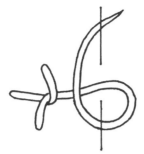

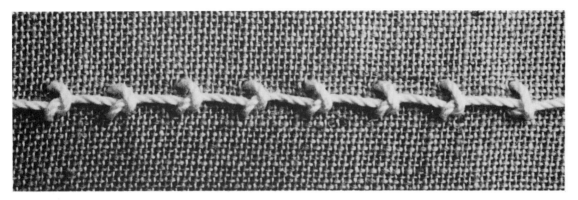

Palestrina stitch

 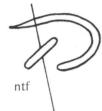  

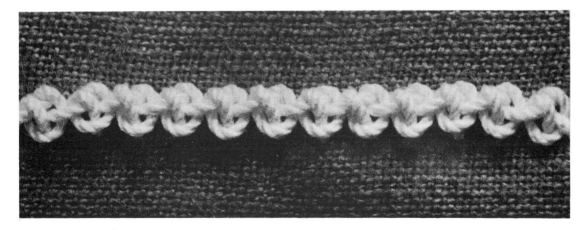

Line sorbello stitch

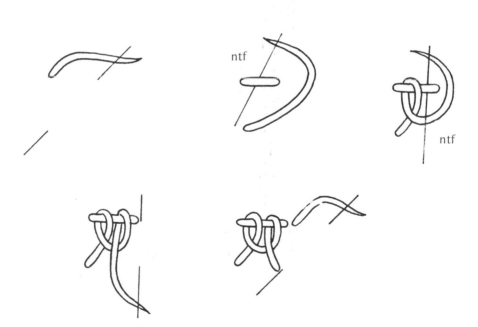

German buttonhole stitch

  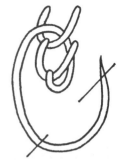

Raised band buttonhole stitch

Buttonhole with extra line stitch

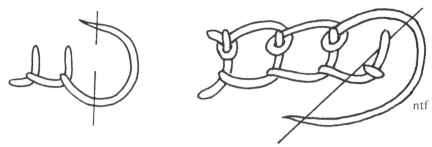

Double overcast stitch

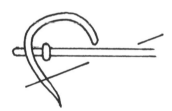
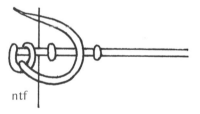

Twin buttonhole stitch

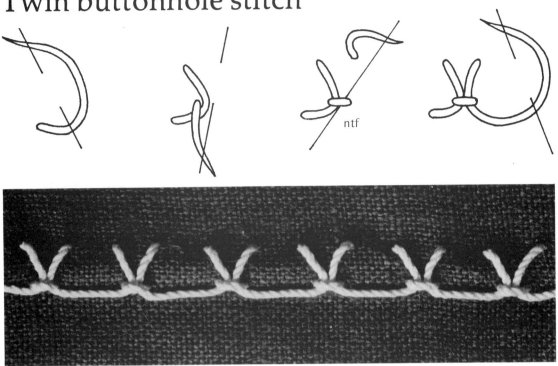

Cross knotted buttonhole stitch

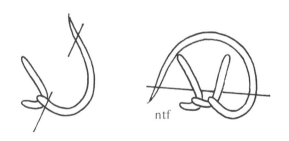

Single and
double knotted buttonhole stitch

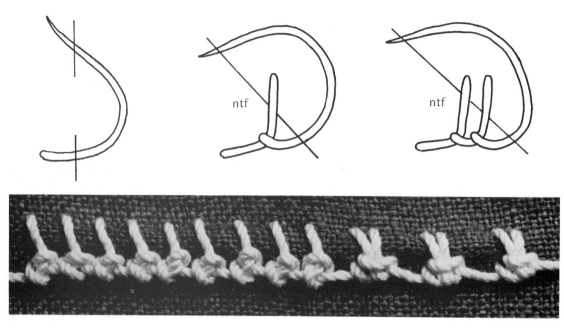

Double buttonhole stitch

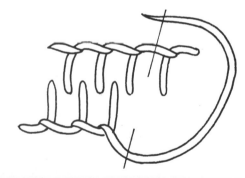

Spiral buttonhole stitch

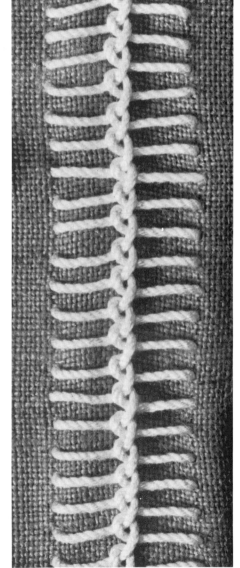

Loop stitch

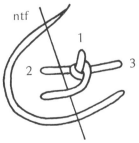

Interlaced buttonhole stitch (1)

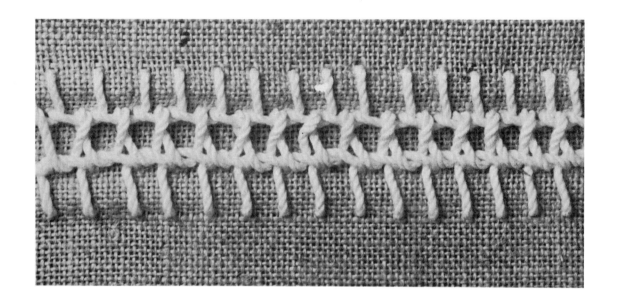

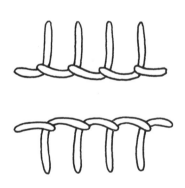

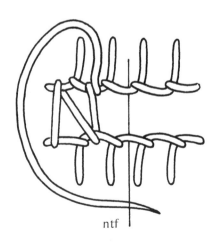

ntf

Interlaced buttonhole stitch (2)

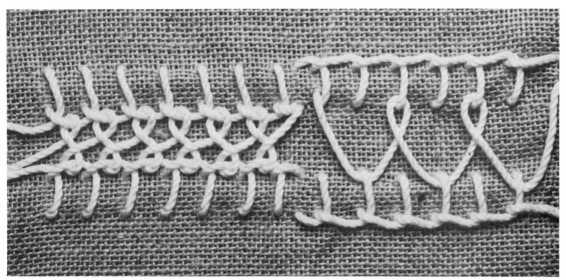

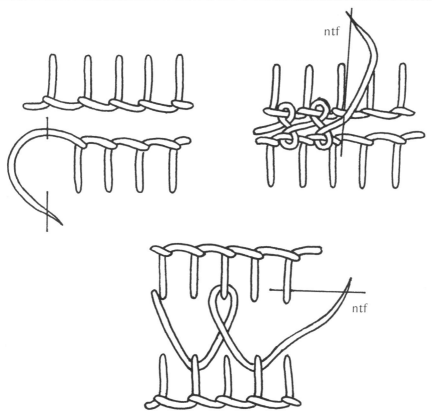

Barb stitch

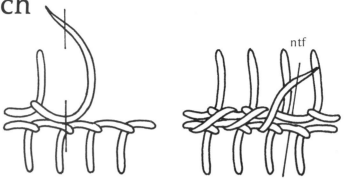

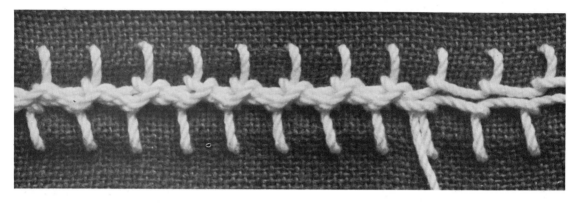

Laced buttonhole stitch

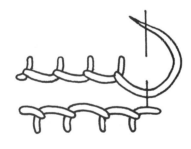
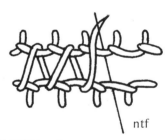

Diamond stitch

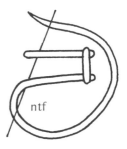
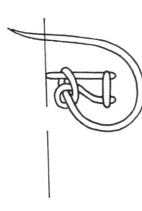

Siennese stitch

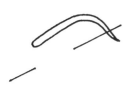

Antwerp edging stitch

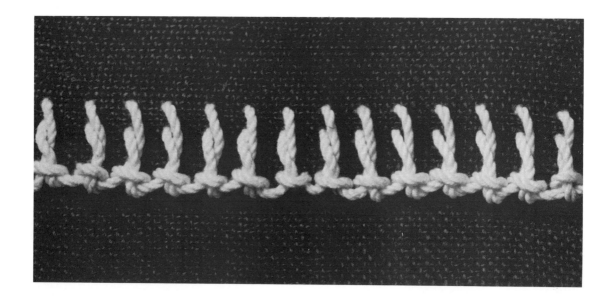

ntf

Laced Antwerp edging stitch

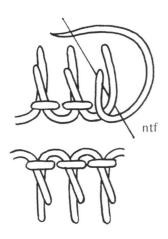

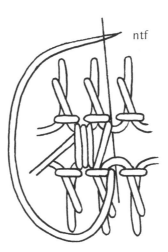

Fringed Antwerp edging stitch

The fringe is put through the loop and pulled down

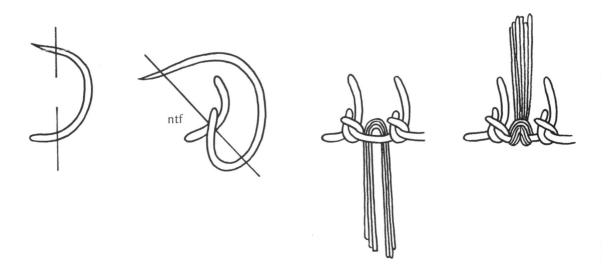

ntf

Buttonholed bar stitch

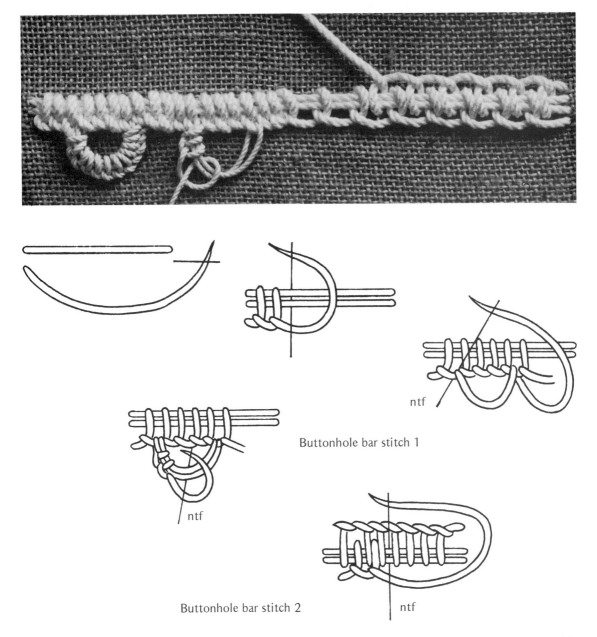

ntf

Buttonhole bar stitch 1

ntf

Buttonhole bar stitch 2   ntf

Loop buttonhole stitch

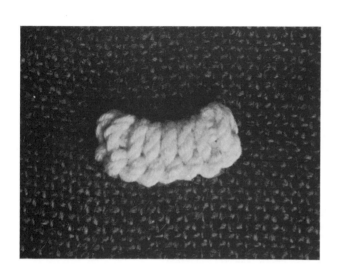

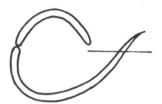

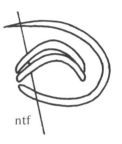

ntf

Point de minute stitch

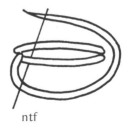

ntf

Raised cup stitch

Continue round the triangle to produce this raised circle

ntf

Catherine wheel

Various centres are worked, in this instance it is a woven wheel

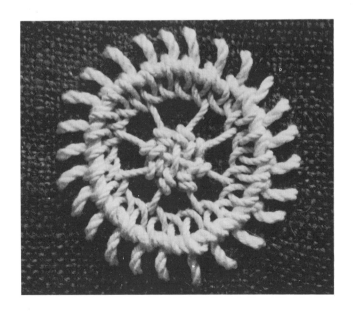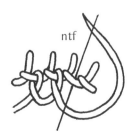

ntf

Wheel buttonhole stitch

A battlement stitch

Stem buttonhole stitch

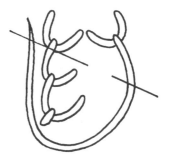

Drawn buttonhole stitch

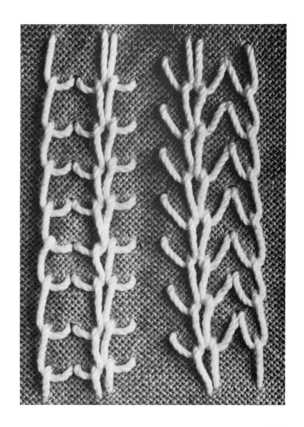

Buttonhole filling stitch

 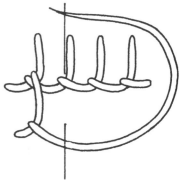

Attached buttonhole stitch

 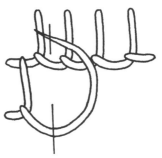

Spaced buttonhole filling stitch

This stitch is always worked from left to right

Fixed

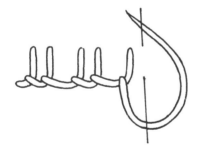

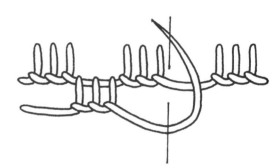

Free

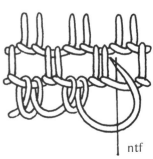

ntf

Rich buttonhole stitch

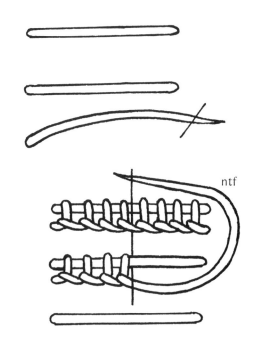

Fancy buttonhole filling stitch

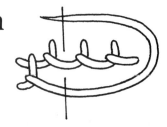

Point de sorrento stitch

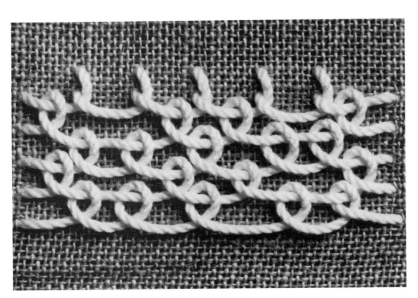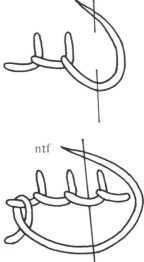

Ceylon buttonhole stitch

The movement is left to right, right to left, left to right etc

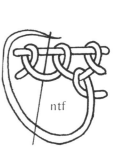

Interlaced running stitch

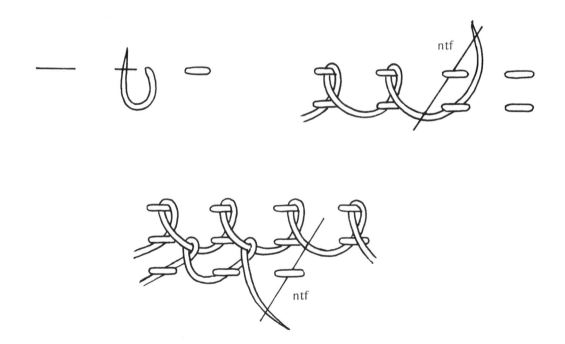

Double buttonhole filling stitch

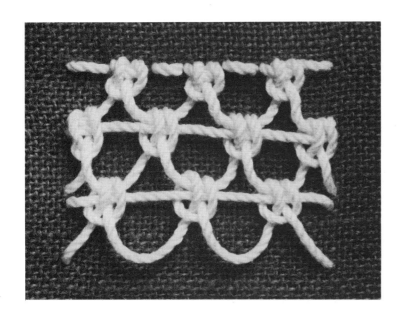

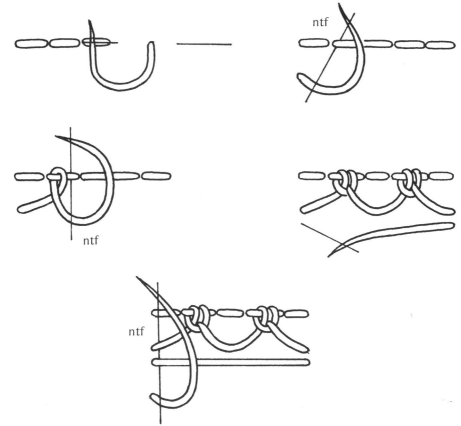

Knotted buttonhole filling stitch

This stitch is worked left to right, right to left, left to right, etc

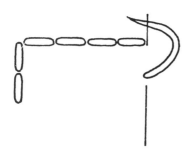

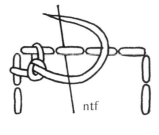

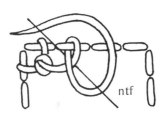

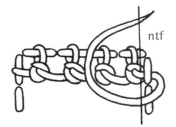

Fancy buttonhole stitch

The first row is left to right, then right to left, left to right, etc

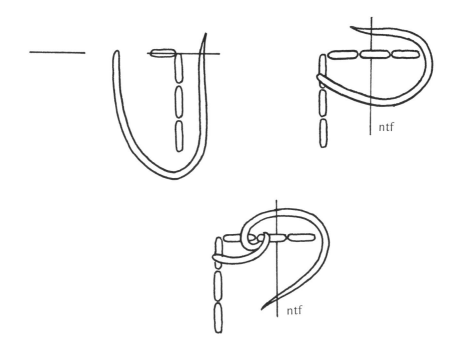

Raised buttonhole stitch

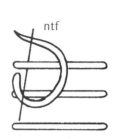

ntf

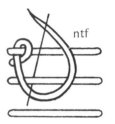

ntf

Couching buttonhole stitch

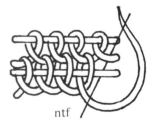

ntf

Detached buttonhole stitch

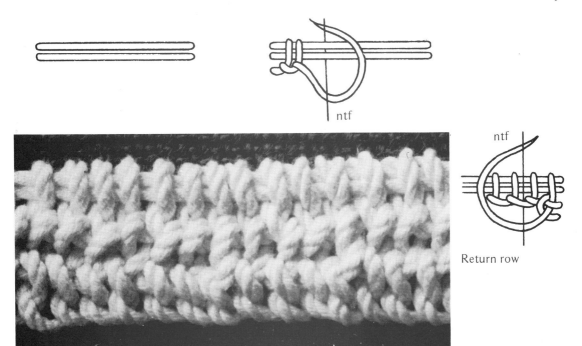

Ceylon stitch

The movement is left to right, right to left etc

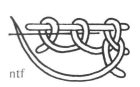

Needle coiling stitch

This stitch is always worked from left to right

Ceylon buttonhole lace stitch

Open buttonhole filling stitch

and lace stitch, which is a variation of this stitch
The movement is left to right, right to left, left to right etc

ntf

Lace stitch

Knotted double buttonhole filling stitch

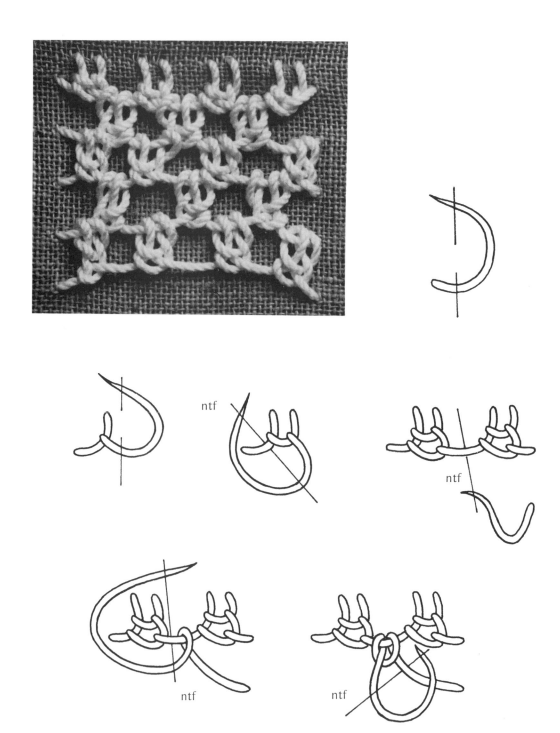

162

Italian buttonhole

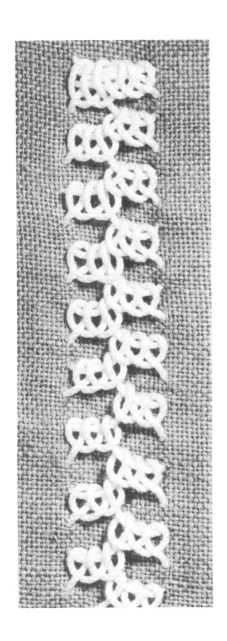

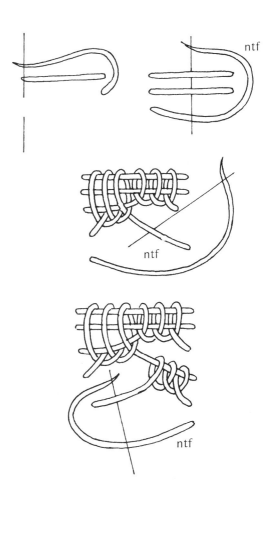

Extra twist buttonhole stitch
and Knot at loop base buttonhole stitch

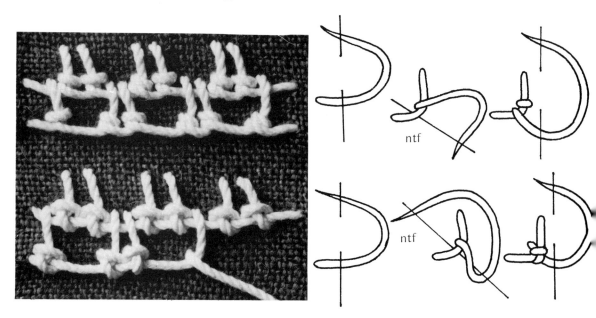

Honeycomb stitch

The thread is twisted around the needle

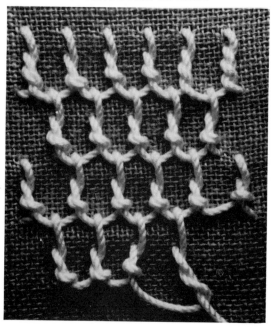

CHAIN STITCHES

Chain stitch

Back stitched chain stitch

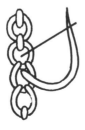

Whipped chain stitch

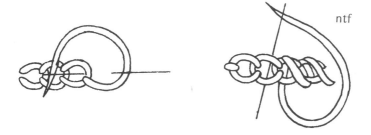

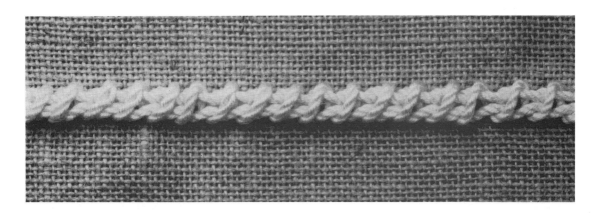

Chain stitch and extra line

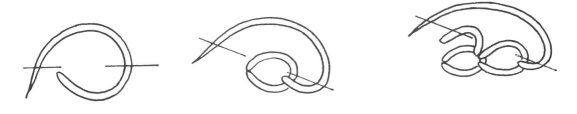

Whipped double chain stitch

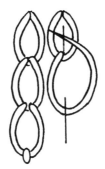
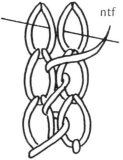

Twisted chain stitch

Coral knot stitch

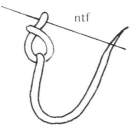

ntf

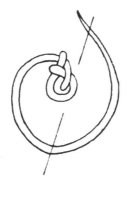

Opposite twisted chain stitch

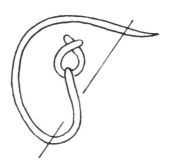

Linked double chain stitch

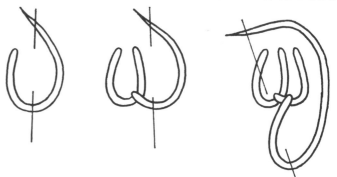

Alternating chain stitch

Upper part of
photograph

Lower part of
photograph

Reverse double chain stitch

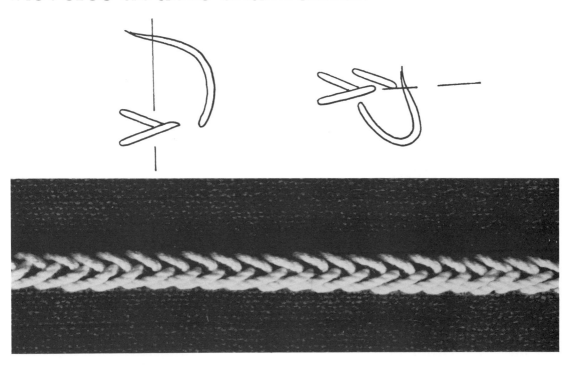

Crossed chain stitch

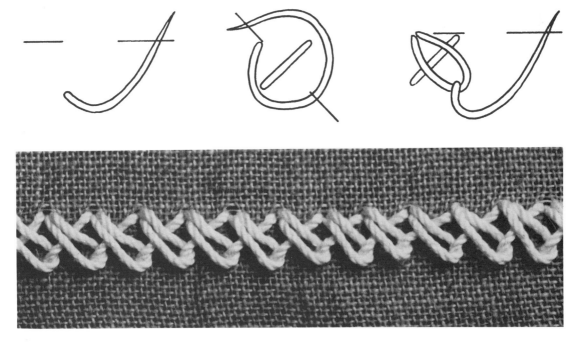

Double chain stitch

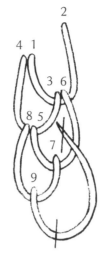

Surprise chain stitch

Detached slip chain stitch

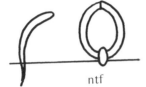

ntf

Spine chain stitch

Broad chain stitch

Open chain stitch

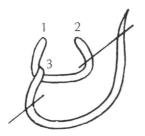

Heavy chain stitch

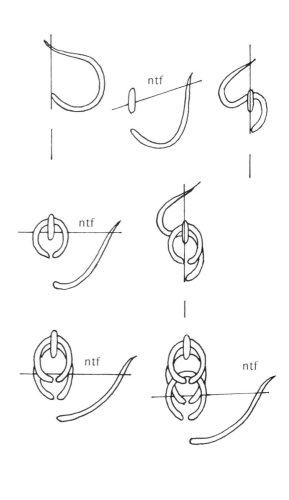

Rosette chain stitch
and circle rosette chain stitch

Come up to start here

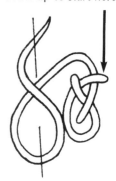

ntf

Braided chain stitch

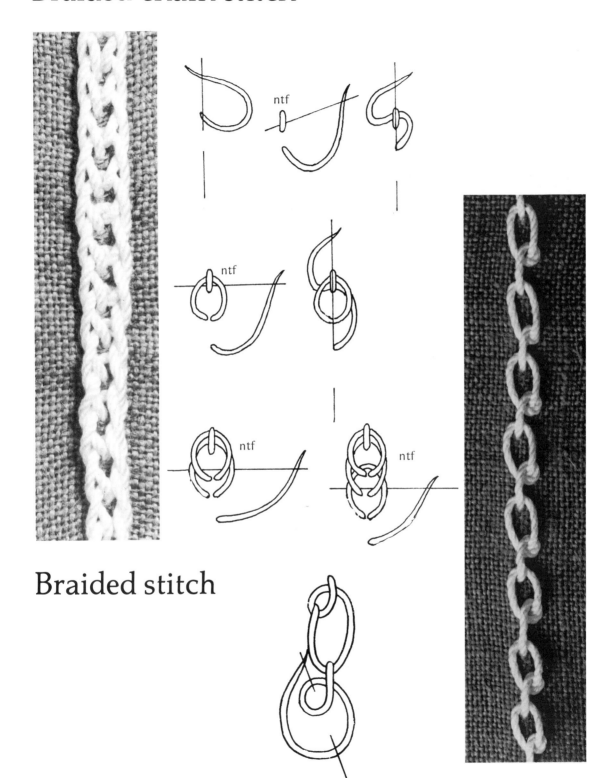

ntf

ntf

ntf

ntf

Braided stitch

Triple chain stitch

The first vertical chain stitch is short, subsequent stitches are longer

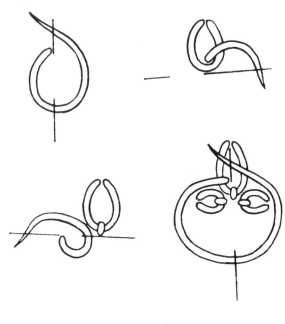

Knotted chain stitch

ntf

Braid stitch

Crested chain stitch

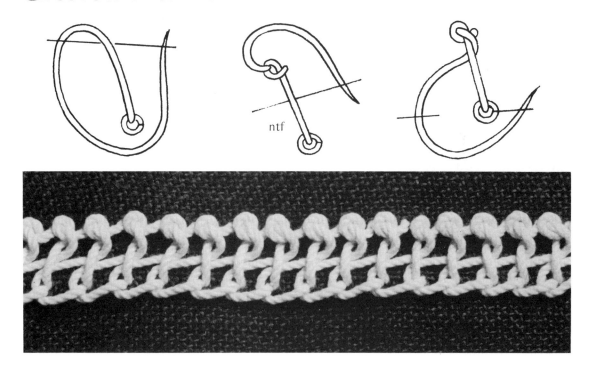

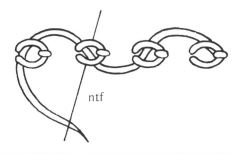

Threaded chain stitch

Pearl stitch

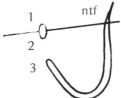

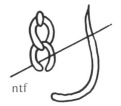

Zigzag chain stitch

Zigzag Spanish knotted stitch

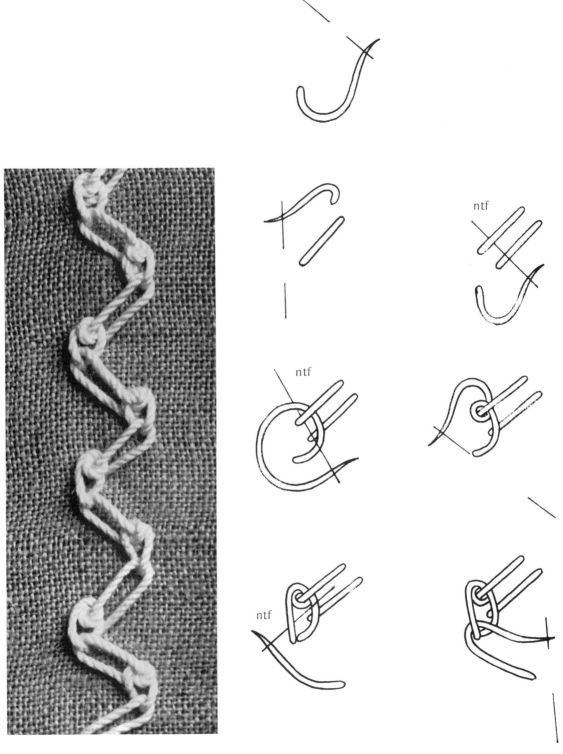

181

Interlaced chain stitch

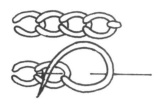 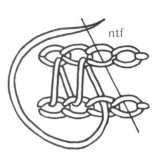

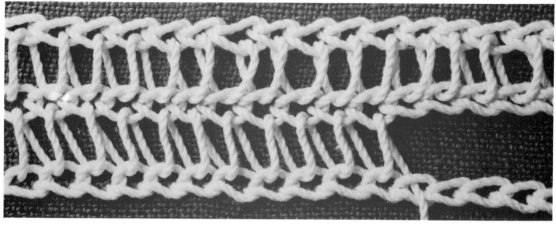

Double cable chain stitch

 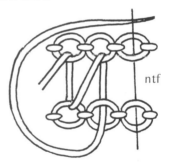

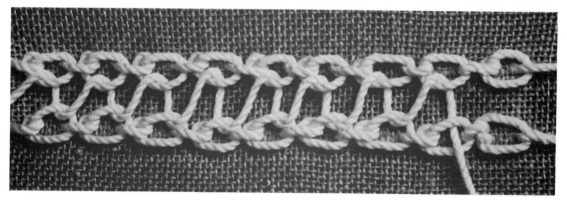

Open trellis stitch

Chain stitch to make surround
ntf except to come up and down

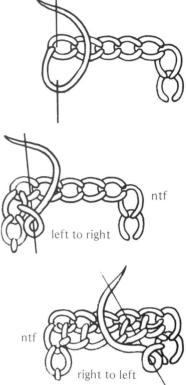

ntf

left to right

ntf

right to left

Trellis stitch

Worked left to right and then right to left

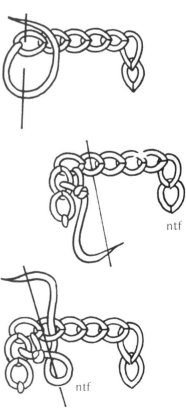

ntf

ntf

Hollie stitch

A chain stitch base

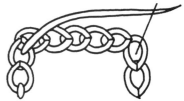
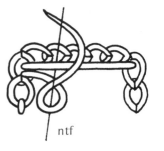

ntf

Double tied open chain stitch

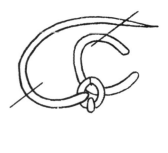

Lace border stitch

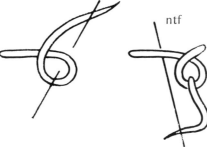

ntf

ntf

Cable chain stitch

Thread twisted around needle once

Rope stitch

This is an exaggerated twisted chain stitch and tension will effect the line produced

Raised rope stitch

Repeat these stages to form the band

Thread twisted
around needle

Snail trail

Knotted cable chain stitch (1)

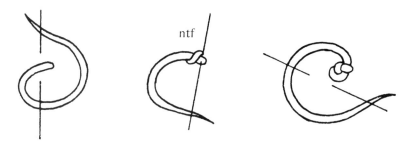

Knotted cable chain stitch (2)

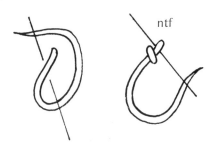

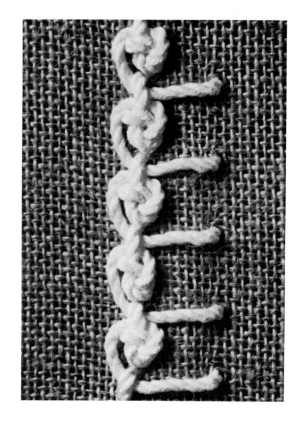

Cable Portuguese chain stitch

Thread twisted around needle

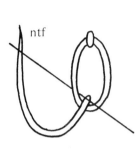

ntf

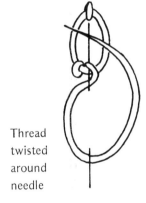

Thread twisted around needle

Slipped cable chain stitch

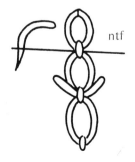

ntf

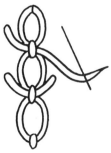

Zigzag cable chain stitch

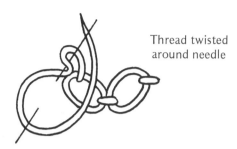

Thread twisted around needle

Zigzag coral stitch

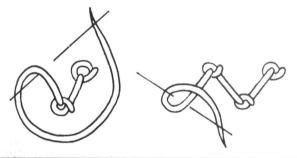

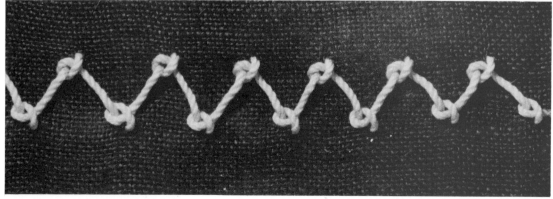

Zigzag crested cable stitch

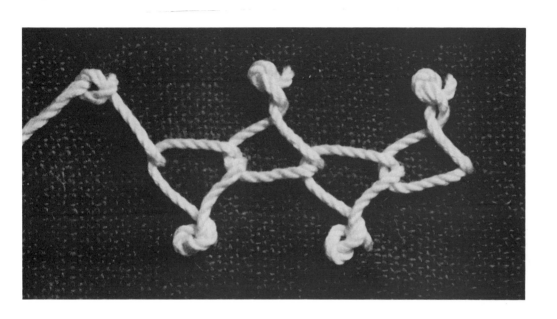

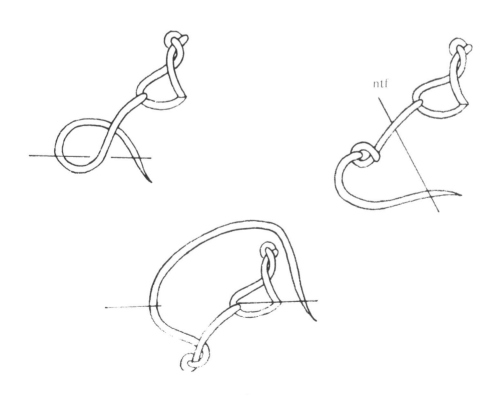

ntf

Tied ladder chain stitch

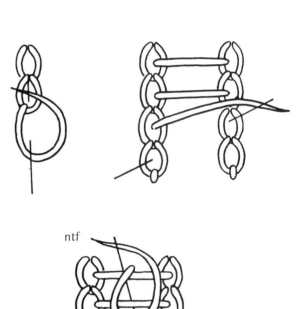

ntf

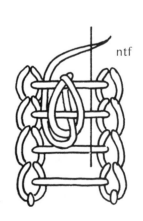

ntf

Step stitch

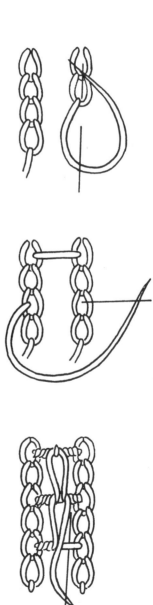

ntf

Linked raised chain band stitch

ntf

ntf

Bar chain stitch

Raised chain band stitch

 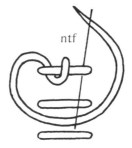

ntf

Butterfly chain stitch

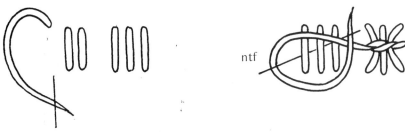

Chained bar

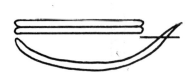 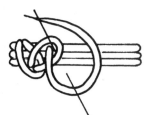 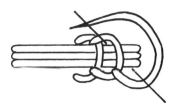

Knotted ground stitch

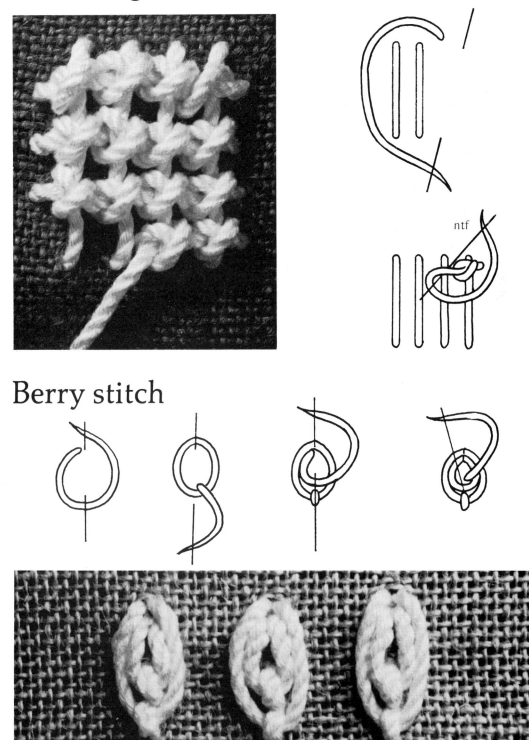

Berry stitch

Russian chain stitch

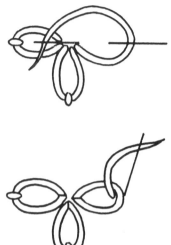

Detached chain stitch

Tulip stitch

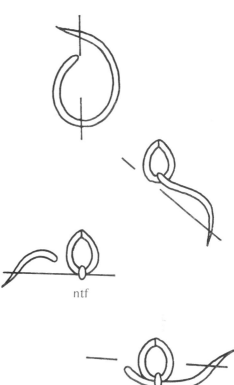

ntf

Three chain stitch

Petal stitch (1)

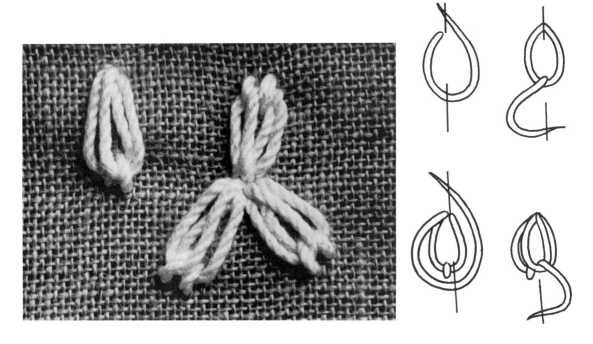

Petal stitch (2)

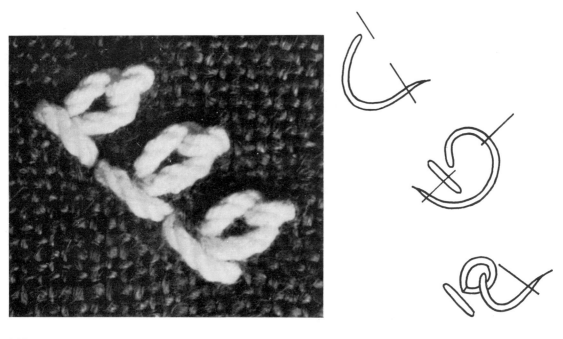

Petal line stitch

Petal wheatear stitch

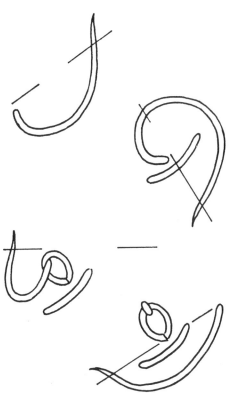

Picot stitch

 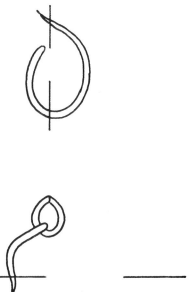

Long tack chain stitch

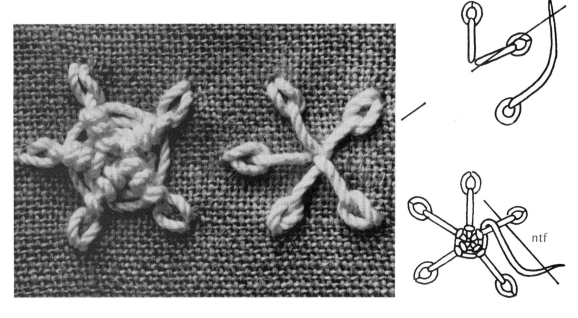

Link powdering

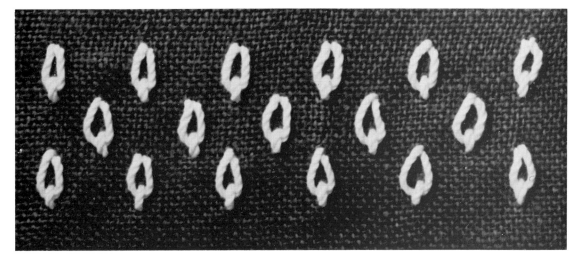

Tête de boeuf filling stitch

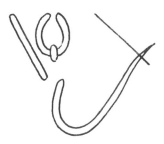

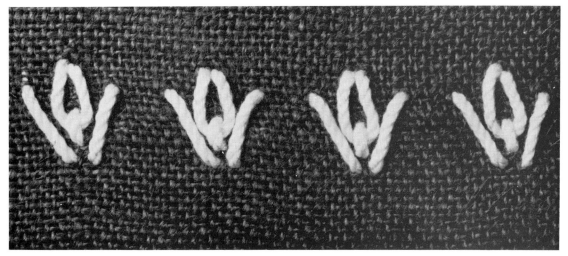

Detached twisted chain stitch

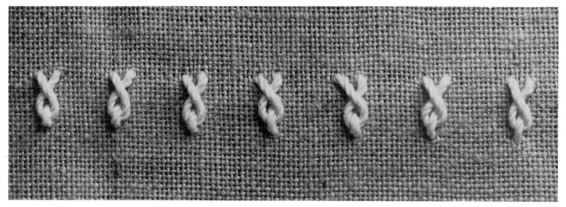

French knot border stitch

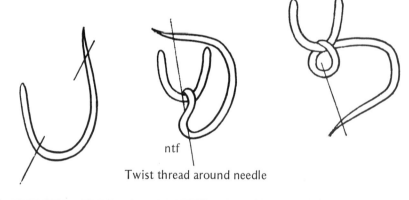

ntf

Twist thread around needle

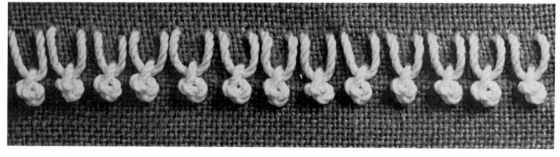

Detached wheatear stitch

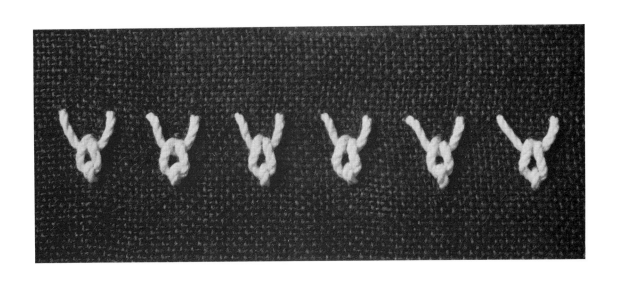

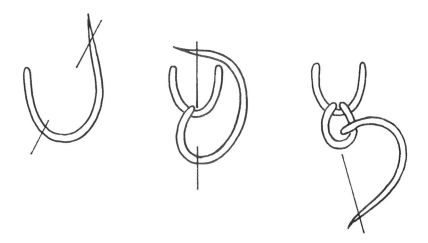

STRAIGHT STITCHES
(INCLUDING CROSS)

French stitch

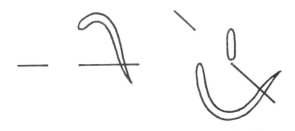

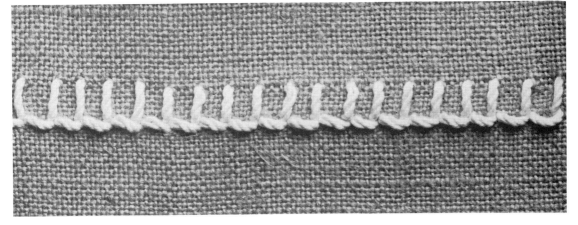

Four sided stitch

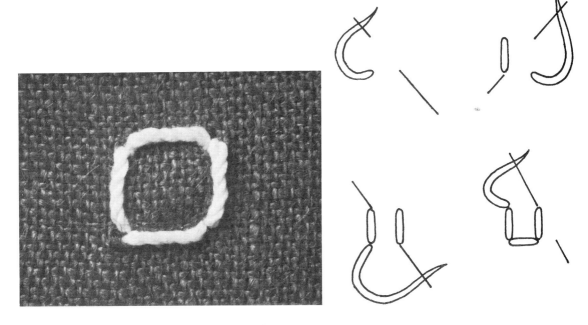

Square stitch

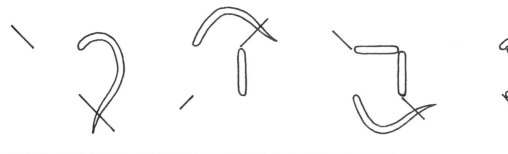

Trellis back stitch

French knot in middle

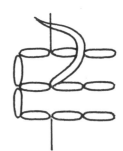

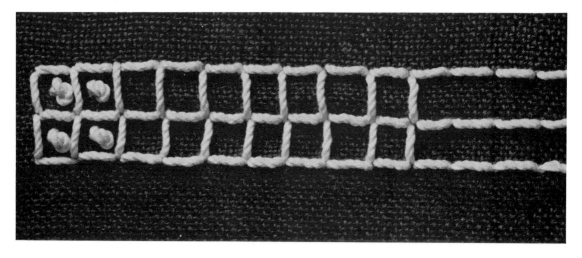

Japanese darning

Italian cross stitch

 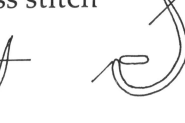

Arrowhead stitch

Order ABCB CDED etc

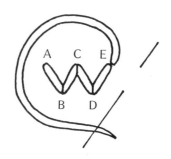

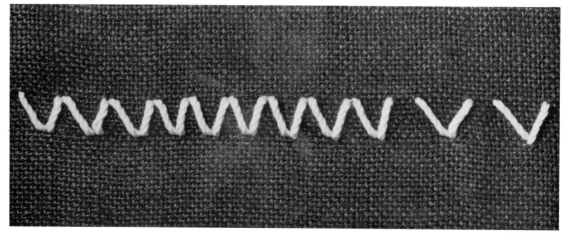

Interlacing over groups of threads

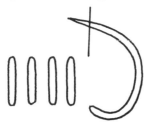 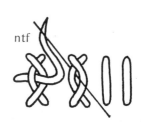

ntf

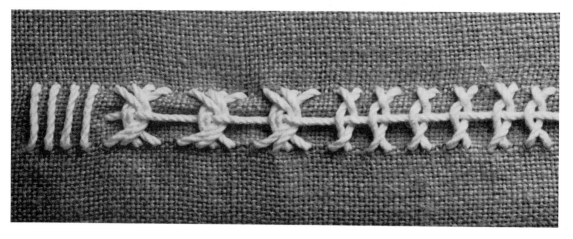

Triangle stitch

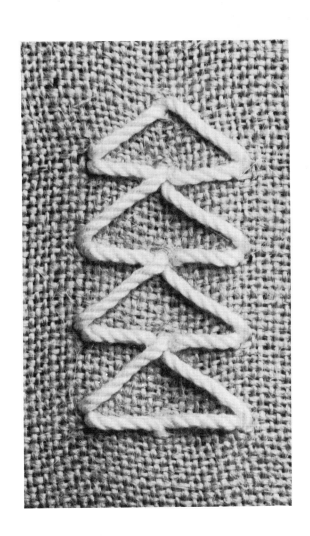

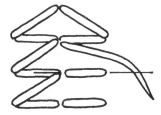

Punch stitch

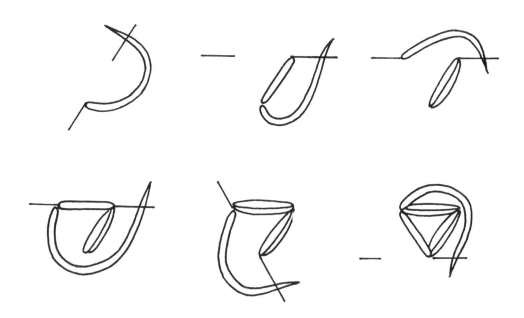

Velvet stitch

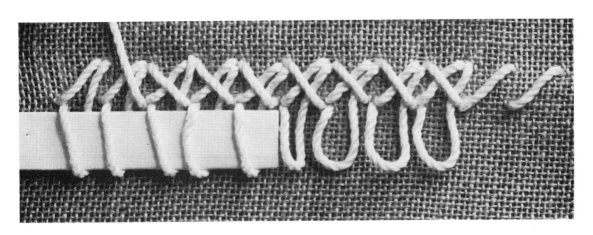

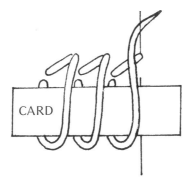

Or each stitch can be completed before moving to the next stitch

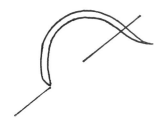

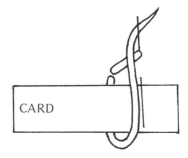

Lock stitch

ntf

ntf

Plush stitch

Turkey work

Needle up here   Needle up here

Dot stitch

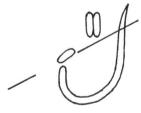

Tent stitch

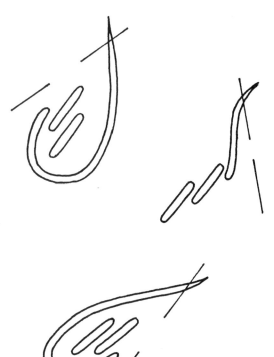

Speckling stitch

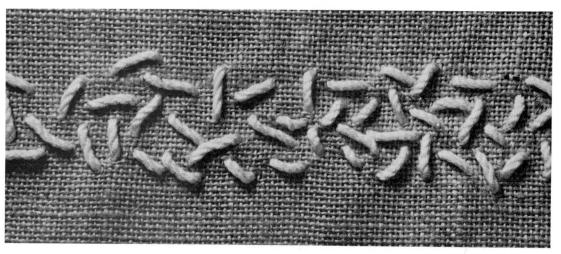

Spaced cross filling stitch

Various patterns can be made by changing the placing
of one cross stitch

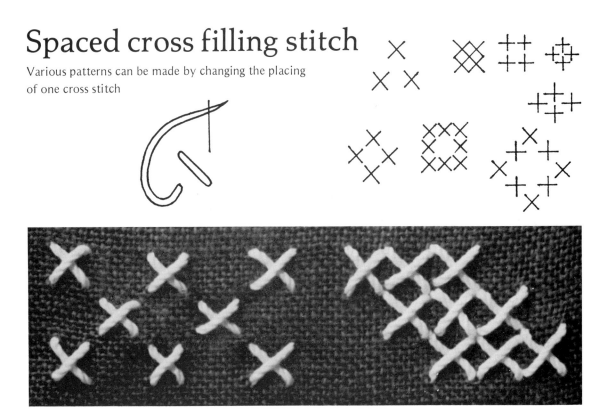

Alternating cross stitch

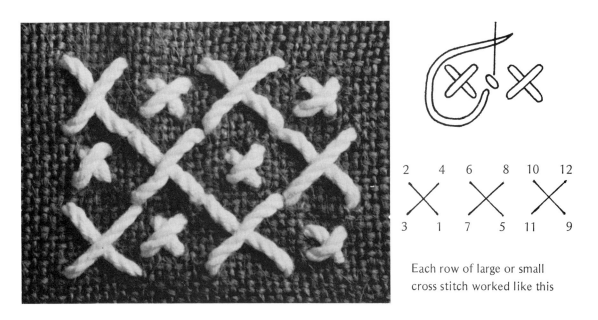

Each row of large or small
cross stitch worked like this

Diagonal filling stitch

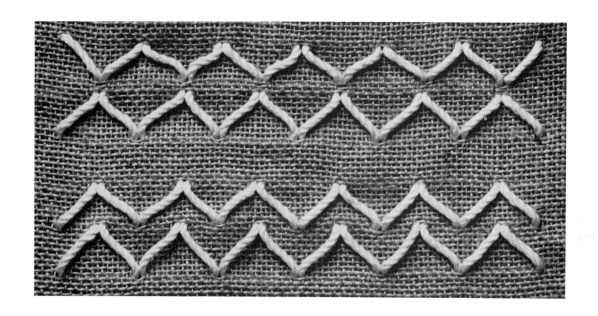

Double border row cross stitch

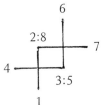

Raised chevron stitch

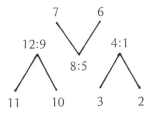

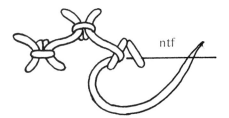

Zigzag stitch

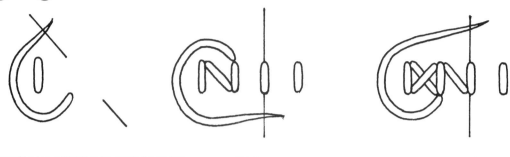

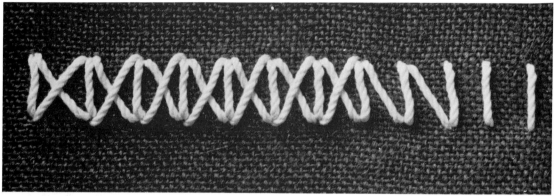

Two-sided cross stitch

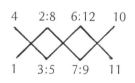

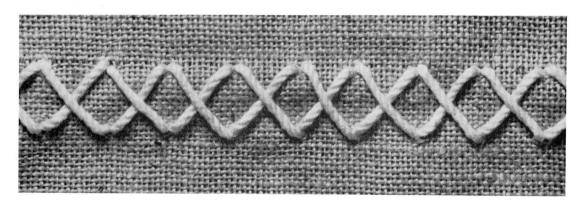

Damask darning

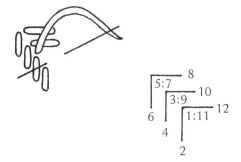

```
       ⌐5:7      8
       |    ⌐3:9   10
    6  |    |  ⌐1:11  12
       4    |   2
```

Soumak stitch

Fishbone stitch
and Open fishbone stitch

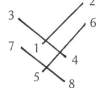

Two-sided plaited Spanish stitch

Flat stitch

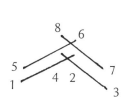

Leaf stitch

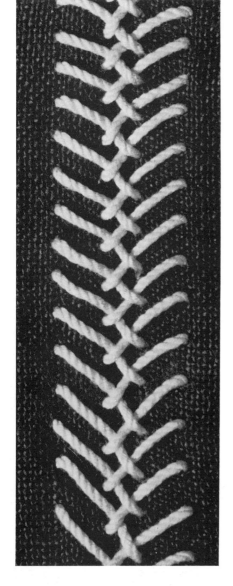

Ship ladder stitch

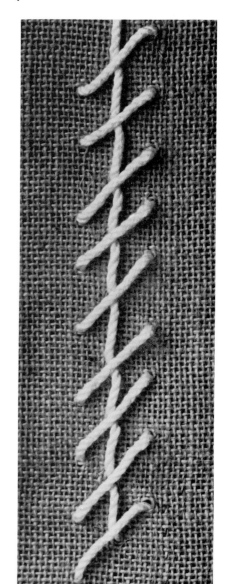

Fern stitch

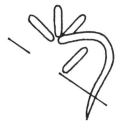

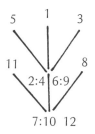

Vandyke stitch

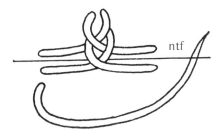

Quill stitch

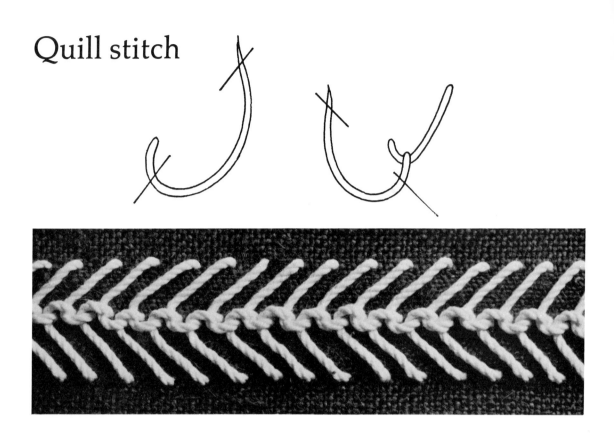

Long armed cross stitch

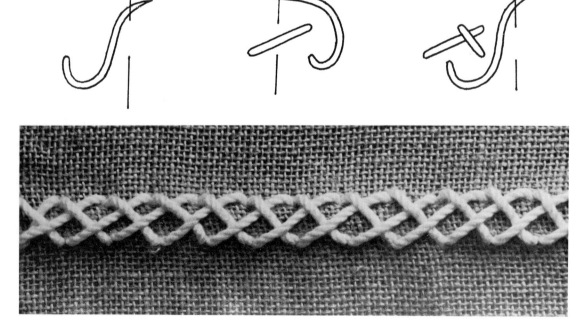

Moorish diagonal cross stitch

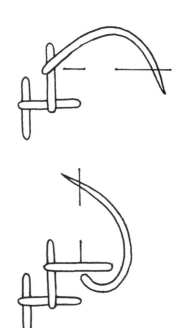

Basket stitch

Thorn stitch

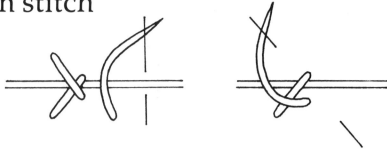

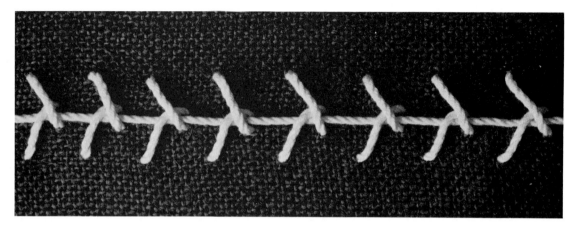

Chevron stitch

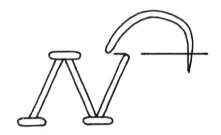

Pagoda chevron stitch

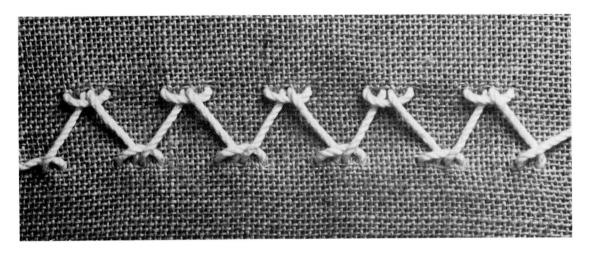

Chess board filling stitch

Sheaf filling stitch

 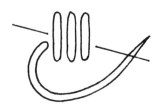

Italian sheaf stitch

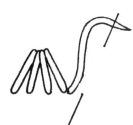

Turn work so that
this row is now the
top

 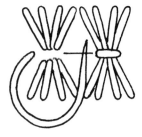

Roumanian filling stitch

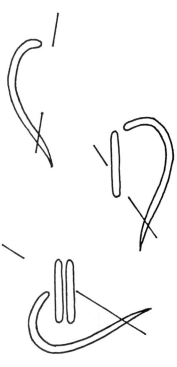

Vell stitch

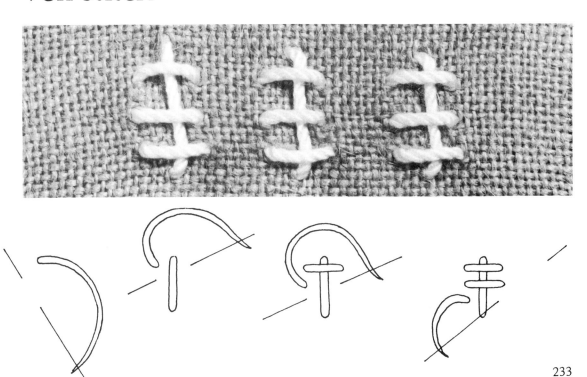

Crossed four stitch

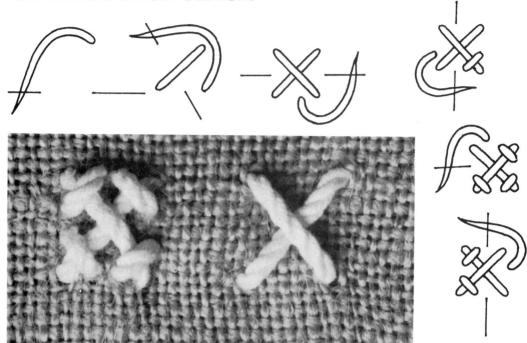

Double cross stitch

Point lance stitch

Star filling stitch

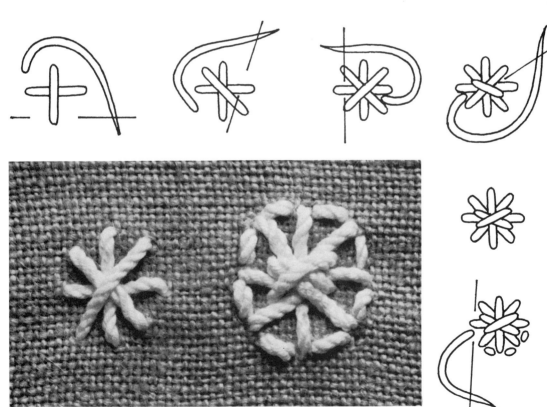

Star stitch

Point russe stitch

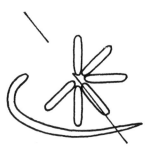

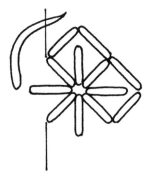

Eyelet filling stitch

Eyelet stitch is the same except that each stage is done twice

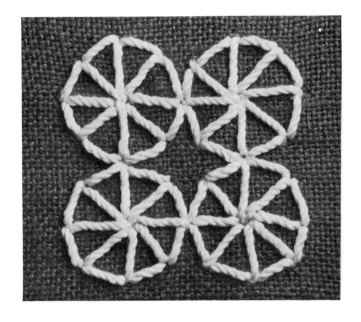

Eyelet stitch

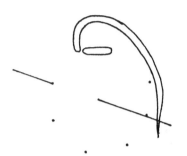

Star of David

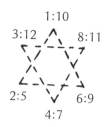

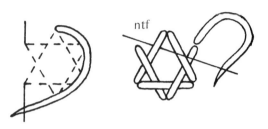

Woven star

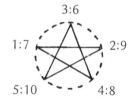

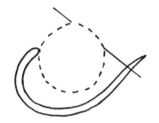

Two-sided insertion stitch

When two motifs are put together a line has to be added

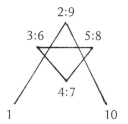

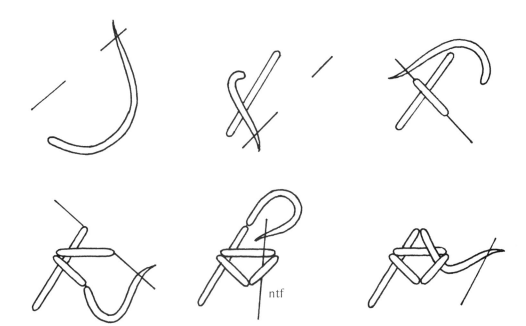

Two-sided triangular Turkish stitch

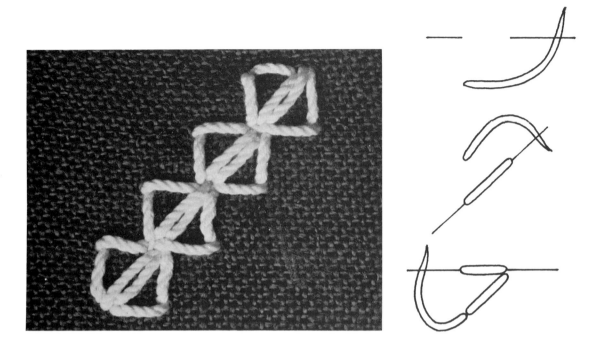

Renaissance stitch

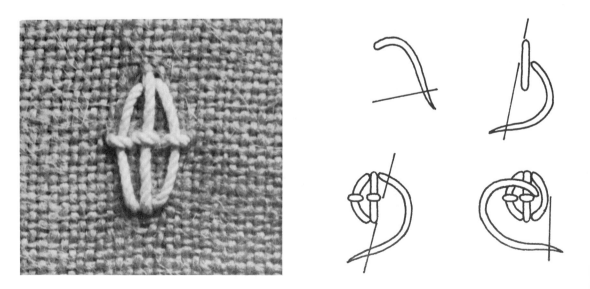

Beetle stitch

Double thread used

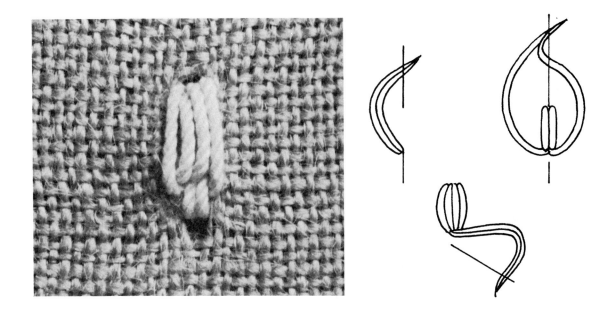

Swedish split stitch

Single thread divided

Oak leaf stitch

Four short stitches are worked into the first stitch

Crown stitch

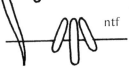

ntf

Knotted cross stitch
and Two trip cross stitch

Knotted cross stitch

Two trip cross stitch

ntf

3:8   2:6

1:5   4:7

Chinese cross stitch

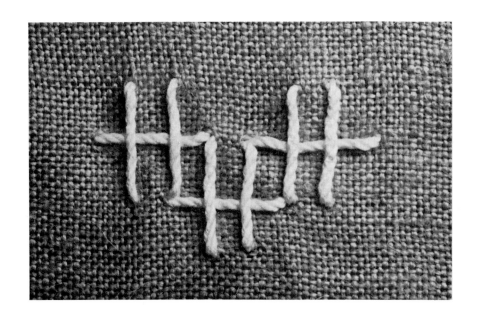

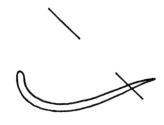

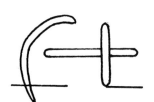

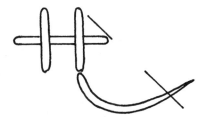

Twisted satin stitch

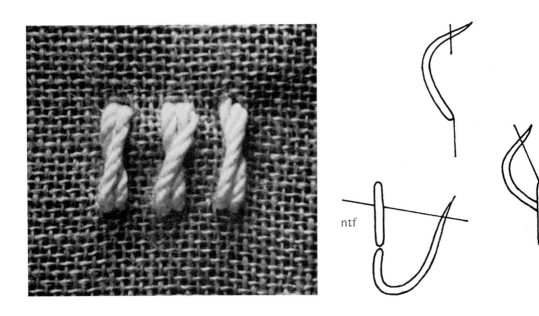

Seeding stitch

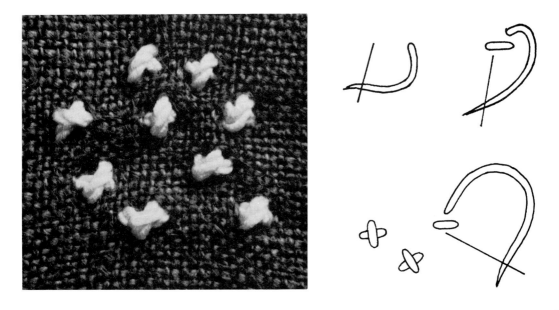

Straight stitch

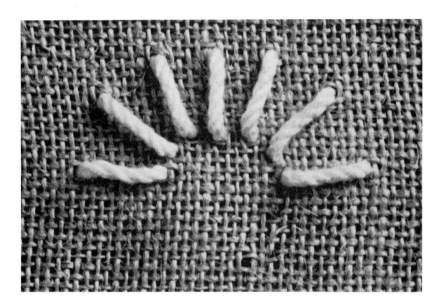

Point Russe stitch

4:5:2:10:6

Crow's foot stitch

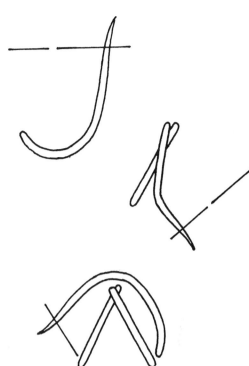

Raised fishbone stitch

Point de vannerie

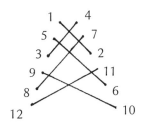

SINGLE UNIT
STITCHES

Ermine filling stitch

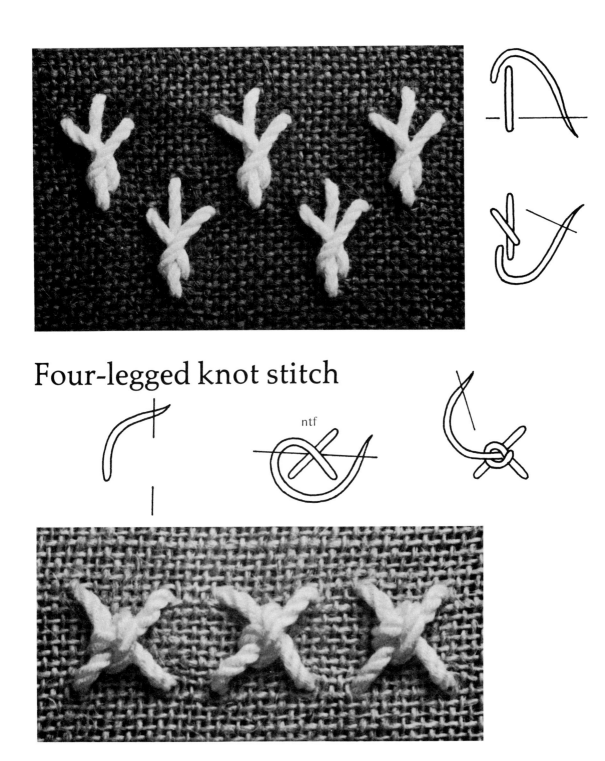

Four-legged knot stitch

ntf

Knotted stitch

  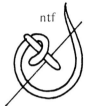

Sorbello stitch

 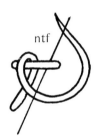 

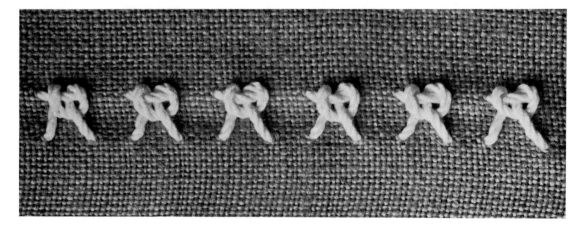

Small edging stitch

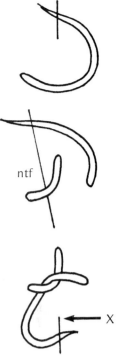

ntf

Needle down at X

Sword edge stitch

Same as small edging stitch, except go down further away from X, at Y

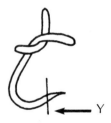

Chain cross stitch

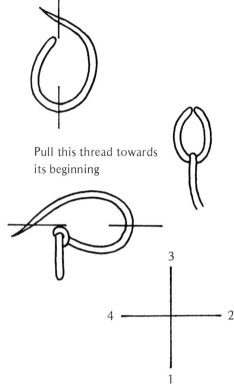

Pull this thread towards its beginning

Cross and twist stitch

ntf

God's-eye stitch

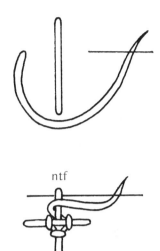

Raised seeding stitch

Rose stitch

Centre for rose stitch, a french knot

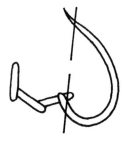

Raised rose stitch

Centre for raised rose stitch, raised seeding stitch

Picot woven stitch

Repeat the last two stages until the weaving is finished
Remove pin from stitch when the stitch is finished
The stitch will then stand up

ntf

ntf

ntf

Woven wheel (1)

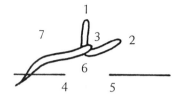

Woven wheel (2)

Stage two worked in a circular direction

Woven wheel (3)

Stage two worked in a clockwise direction

Raised woven wheel

As for woven wheel 2, except a thread is held from the top (as shown here) while the stitch is being worked
The wheel is raised by this action
The thread is removed when the stitch is finished

Ringed spider web stitch

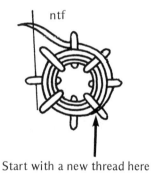

ntf

Start with a new thread here

Bullion stitch

Twist the thread around the needle

Bullion bar stitch

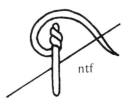

ntf

Raised needleweaving

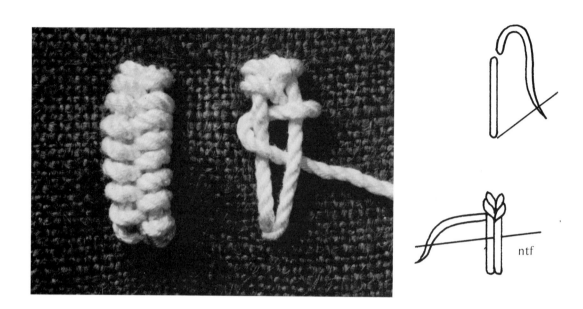

Point à la minute

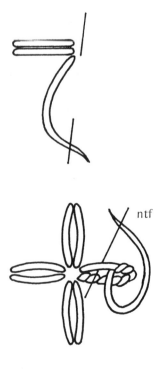

Interlaced cross stitch

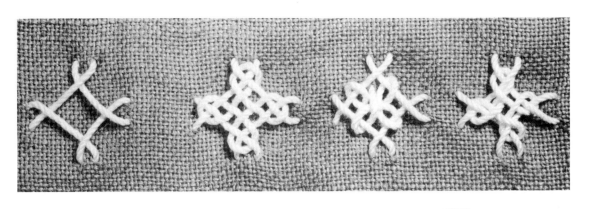

Shisha stitch

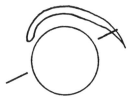

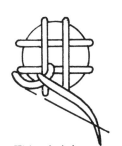

This stitch is
made at the four
points where the
threads cross

Leaf stitch

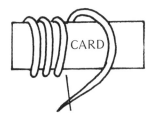

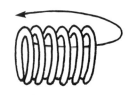

Pull this loop through and back

Turk's head knot

When this knot is formed in this way, go down at point X

Chinese knot

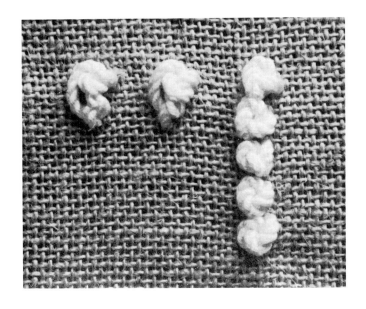

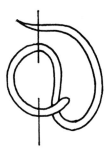

French knot
and French knot stalks

Go down into the fabric at X for a french knot, or further away, at Y,
if french knot stalks are to be produced

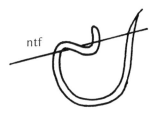

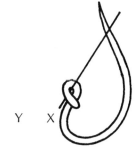

The thread is twisted around the needle

EDGINGS

Looped edging stitch

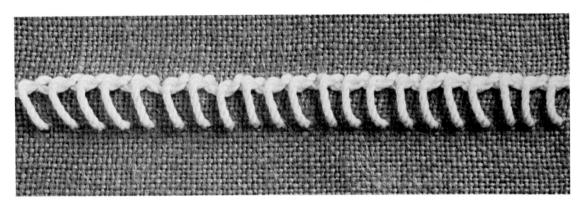

Chevron half stitch

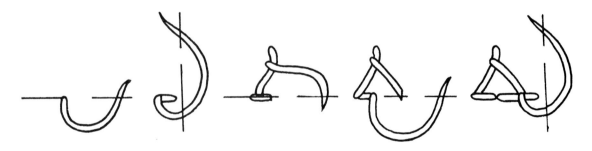

Armenian edging stitch

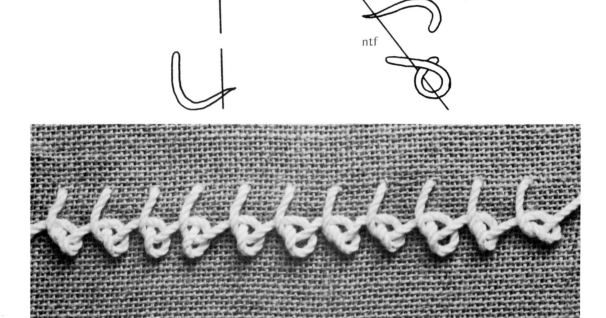

Montmellick stitch

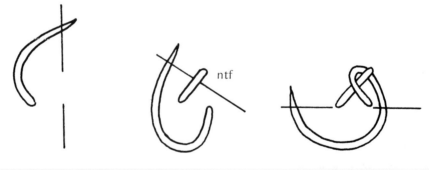

Sailor edge stitch

X = Hold here with left hand thumb

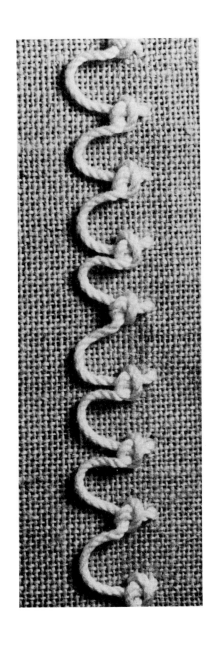

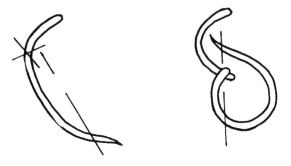

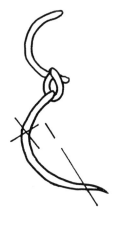

Run fringe

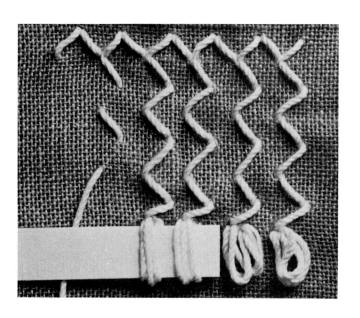
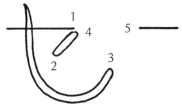

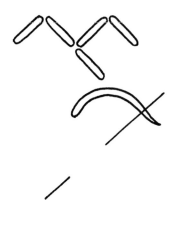
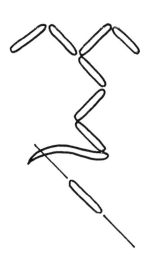
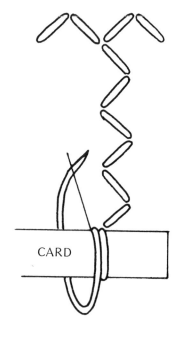

Fancy bobbin edging stitch

FILLING STITCHES

Filling stitch

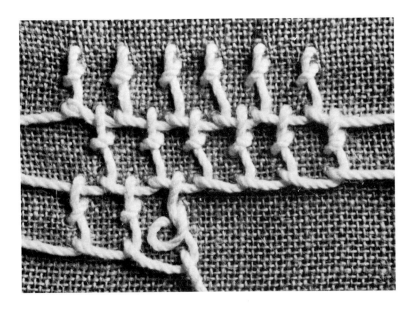

Lace filling stitch

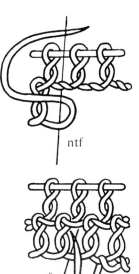

Valsesian stitch

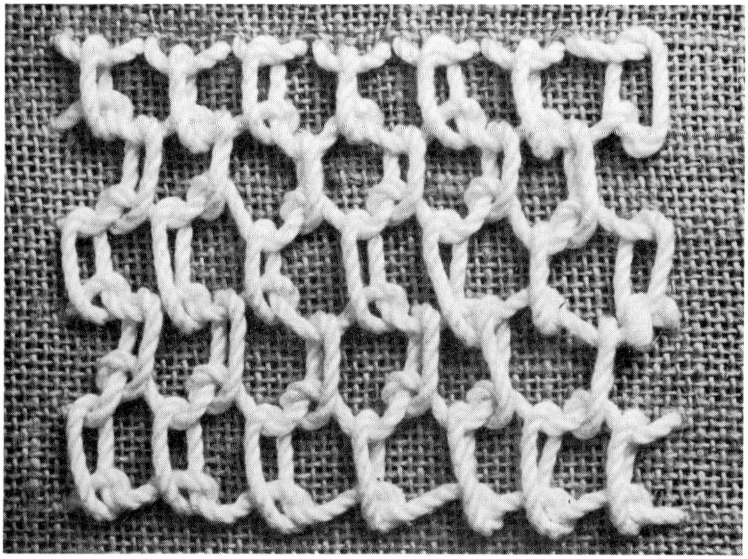

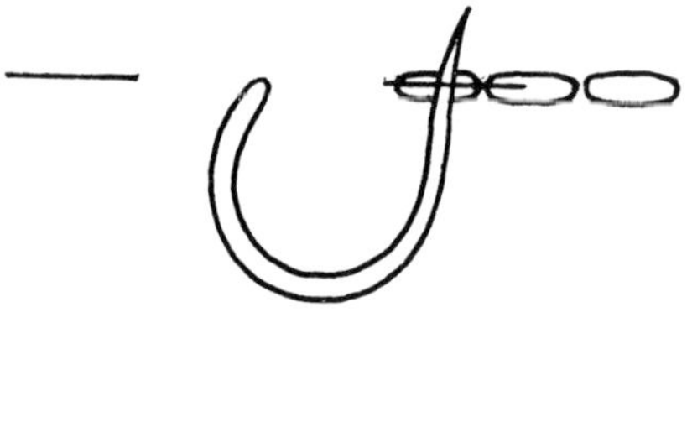

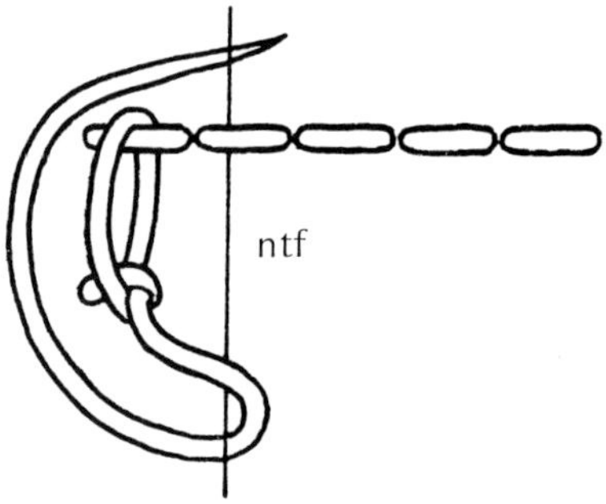

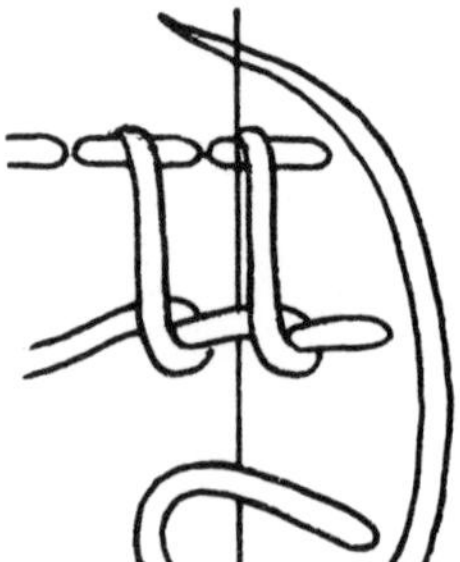

Diamond filling stitch

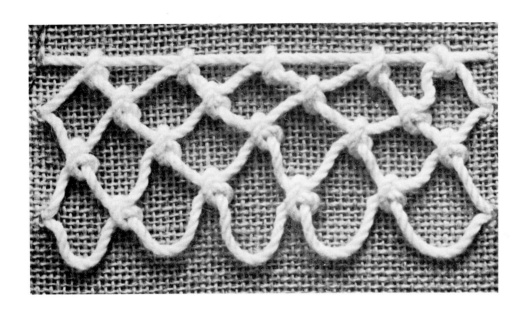

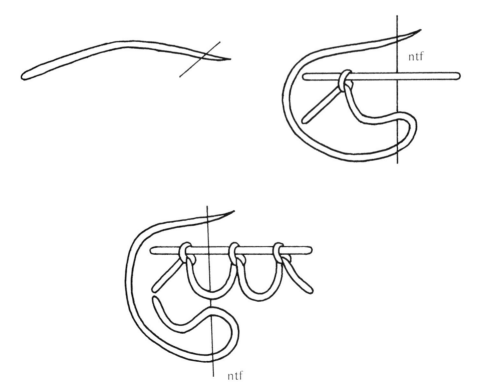

Diamond filling stitch with bars

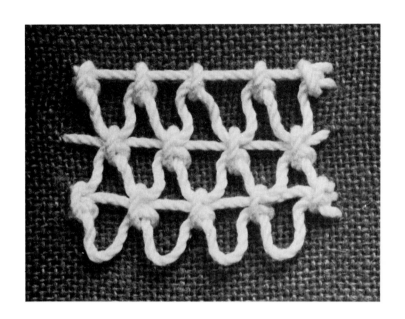

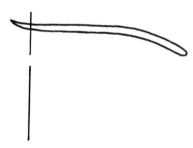

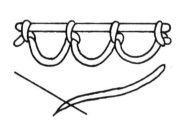

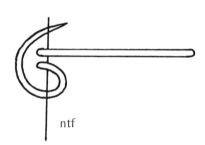

ntf

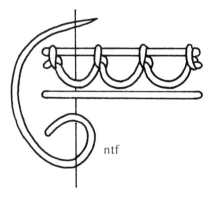

ntf

Filet stitch

Do not pull thread too tight

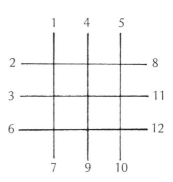

Eastern buttonhole stitch

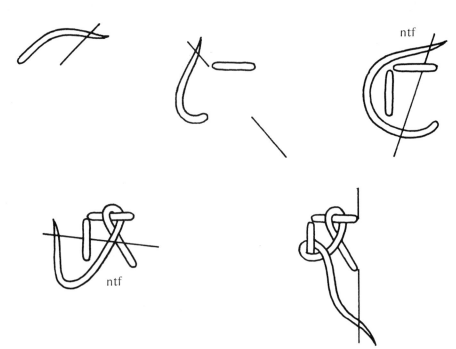

Diamond stitch

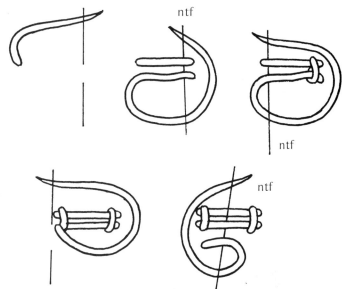

Loop stitch

Free loop is held by the following loop

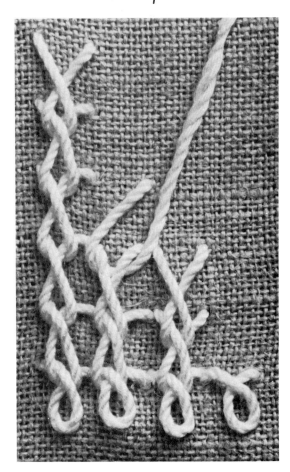

Brick stitch

This stitch is often much closer

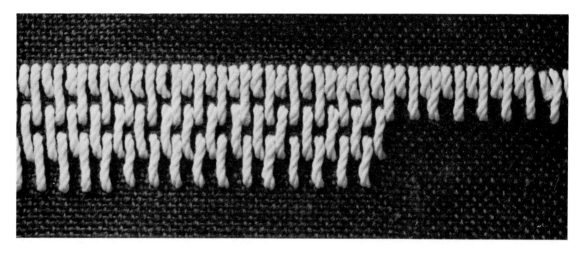

Guilloch stitch

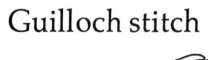

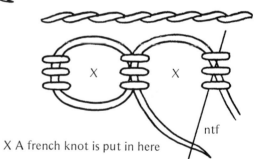

X A french knot is put in here

ntf

Fancy stitch

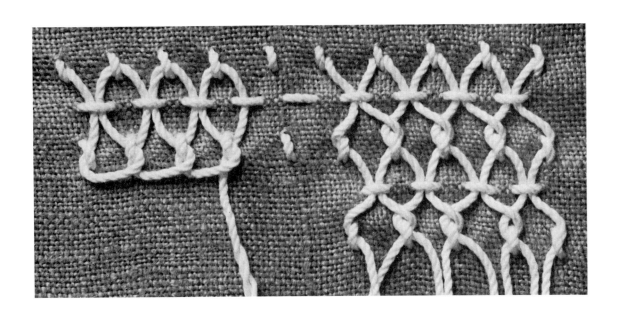

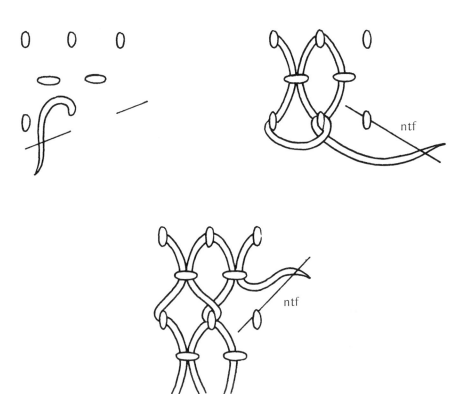

Open and closed wave stitch

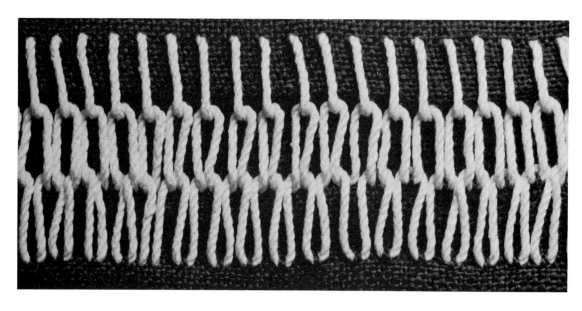

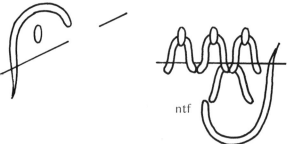

ntf

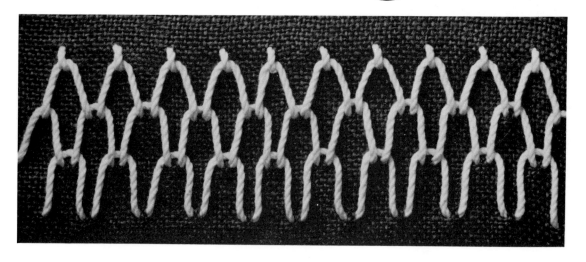

Cloud filling stitch

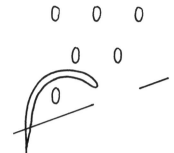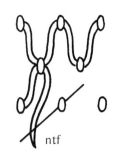

Maltese cross stitch

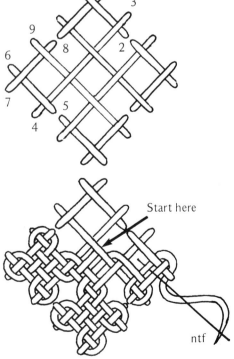

Laced lattice filling stitch

Base as for twisted lattice stitch

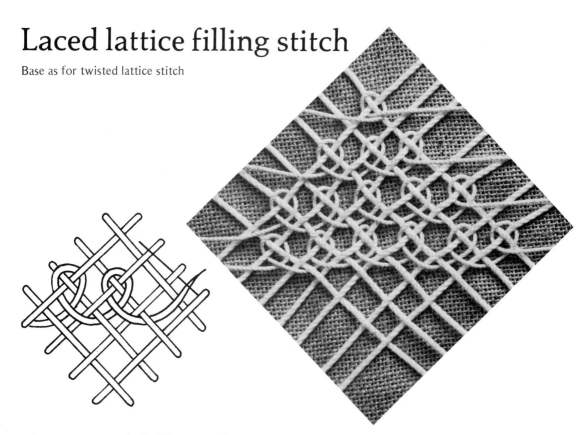

Squared filling base stitch

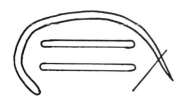

Twisted lattice stitch

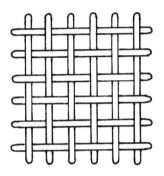

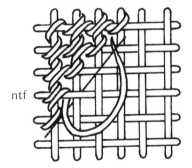

ntf

Detail

Squared filling stitch (1)

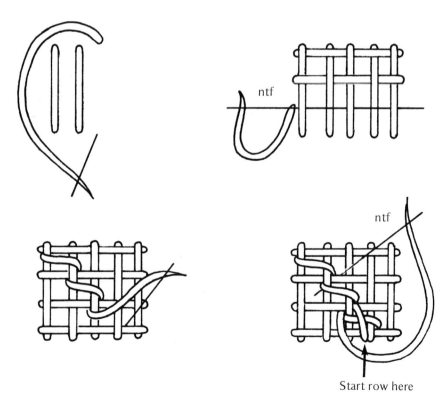

ntf

ntf

Start row here

Squared filling stitch (2)

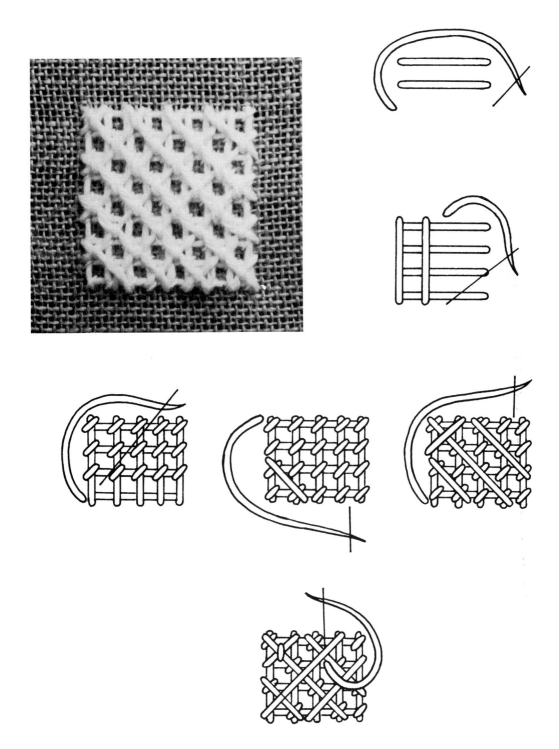

Squared filling stitch (3)

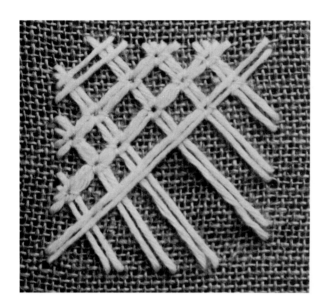
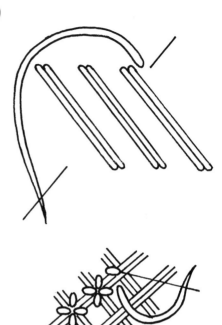

Japanese stitch

Griffin stitch

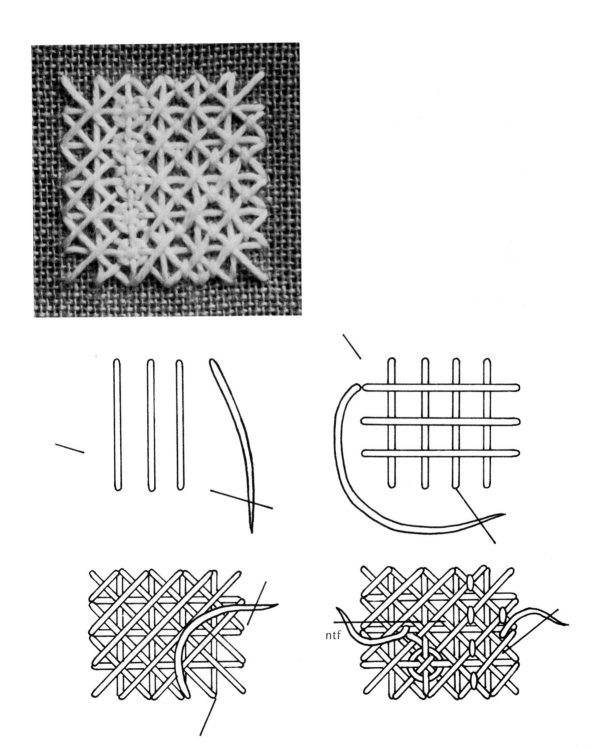

ntf

Long and short satin stitch

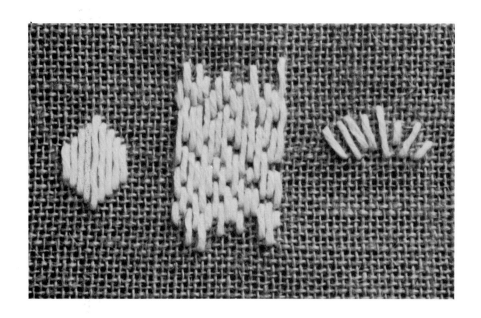

Satin stitch

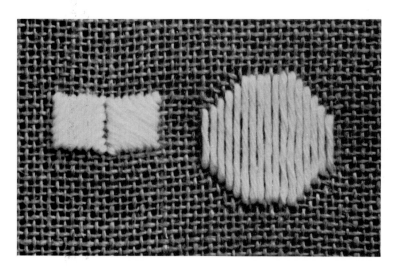

Satin stitch patterns

Raised satin stitch

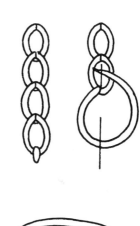

Satin stitches

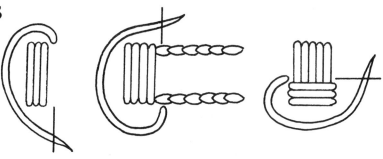

Whipped satin stitch

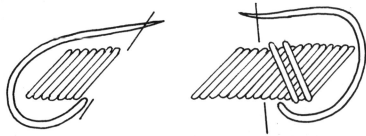

Woven bar stitch

Woven bar stitch with simple picot

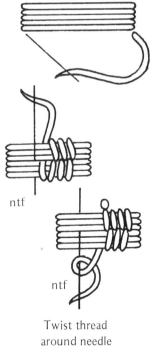

ntf

ntf

Twist thread
around needle

Corded bar stitch

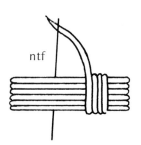

ntf

Faggot filling stitch

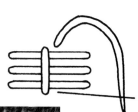

Base faggot filling stitch

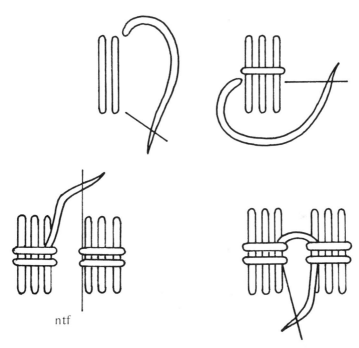

ntf

One-sided insertion stitch

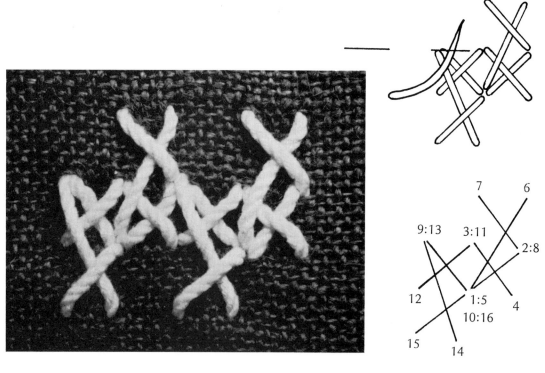

Wrapped cross stitch

Brick and cross filling stitch (1)

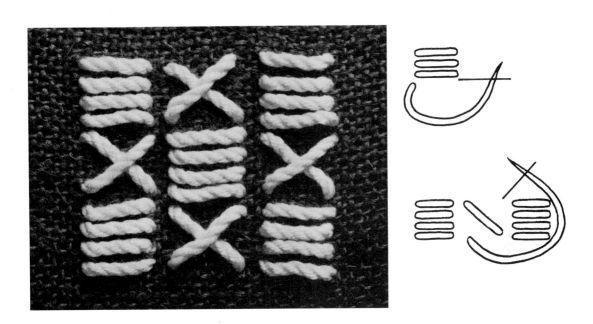

Brick and cross filling stitch (2)

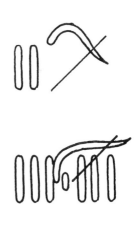

Basket filling stitch

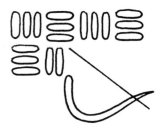

Block stitch

Satin stitch filling squares

This movement is also for satin stitches, satin stitch patterns,
long and short stitch, straight stitch

Bricked stitch

Open filling satin stitch

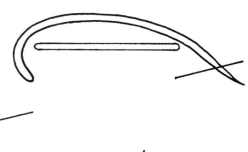

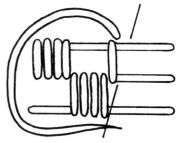

Plaited stitch

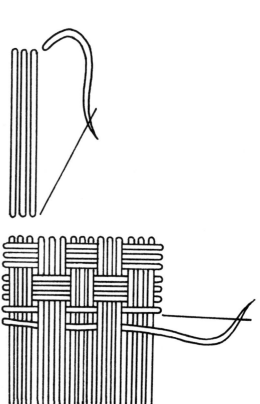

Surface darning stitch

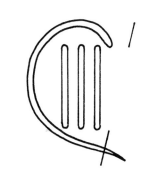

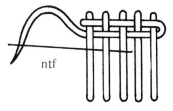

Darning stitch

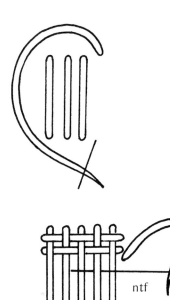

Raised honeycomb filling stitch

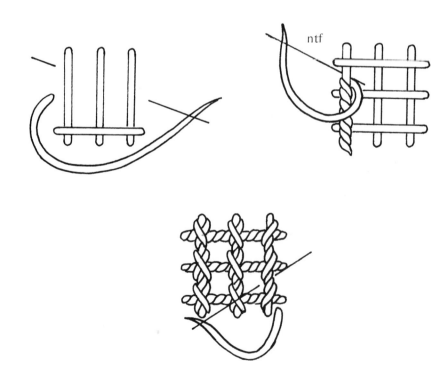

Basket stitch

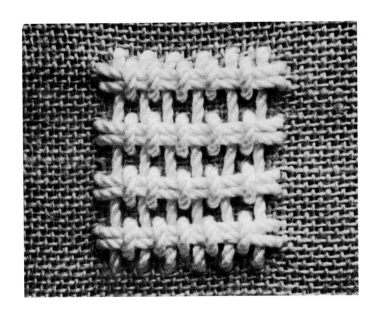

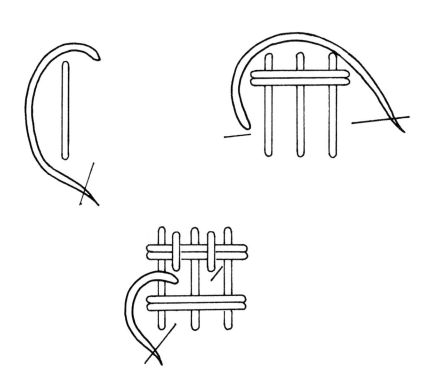

Burden stitch

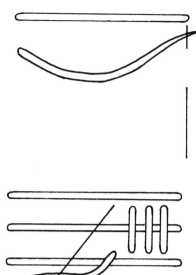

Filling row

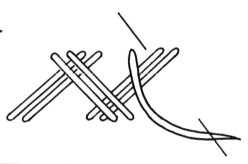

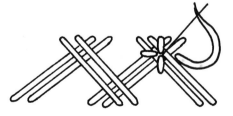

Couched filling stitch

Trellis couching — a variety of stitches holding down this base

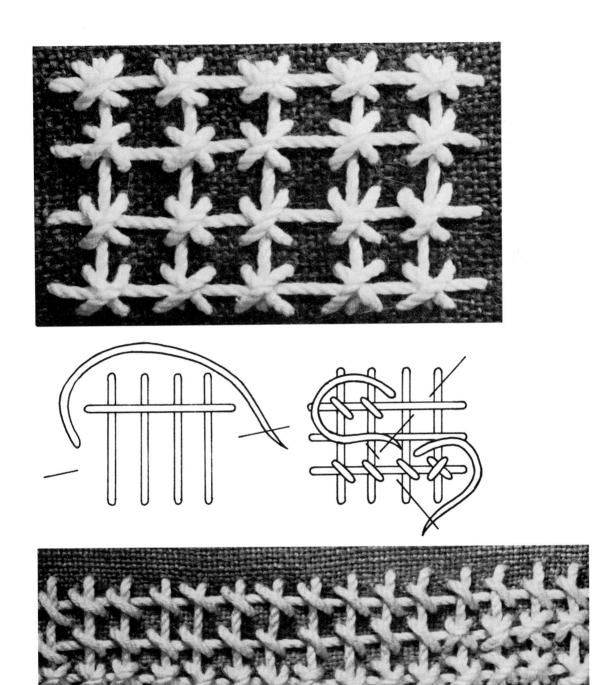

Couched cross filling stitch

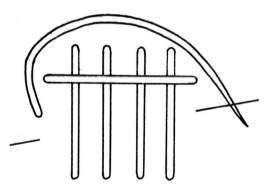

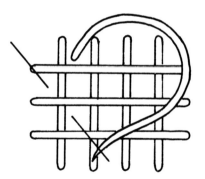

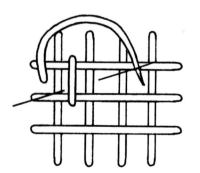

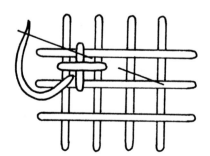

Trellis stitch

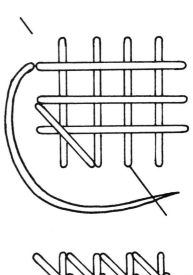

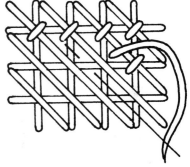

Raised honeycomb filling stitch

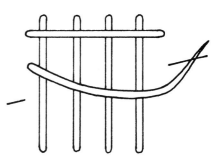

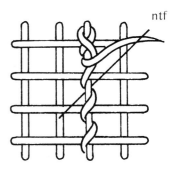

ntf

Star darn

Satin stitch in centres

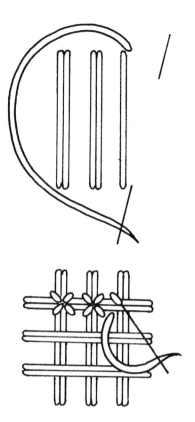

Square filling stitch

French knots in centres

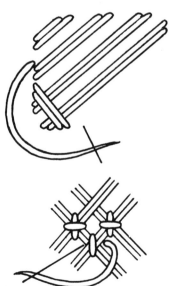

COLOUR PLATES

Colour Plate 1

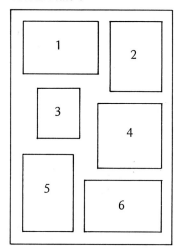

Key

Colour Plate 1
1 Raised buttonhole on a raised band
2 Surface and patterned darning
3 Raised couched filling basket stitch
4 Squares and bundles
5 Diamond oriental filling
6 Satin stitch chevron filling

Colour Plate 2
1 Battlement couching
2 Shaded stem stitch filling
3 Honeycomb filling stitch
4 Chevron filling
5 Block shading
6 Long and short shading stitch

Colour Plate 3
1 Plaited feather stitch
2 Singalese chain
3 Diagonal woven band
4 Striped woven band
5 Patterned couching

Colour Plate 4
1 Triple herringbone stitch
2 Triple couching stitch
3 Persian border couching stitch
4 Double herringbone stitch
5 Laced double running stitch

Colour Plate 5
1 Checked chain band stitch
2 Chequered chain stitch
3 Interlaced chain stitch
4 Fancy couching

Colour Plate 6
1 Darning huckaback
2 Fancy darning stitch
3 Plaid filling
4 Patterned darning weaving

Colour Plate 2

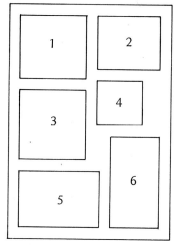

Colour Plate 3

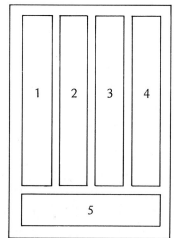

Colour Plate 4

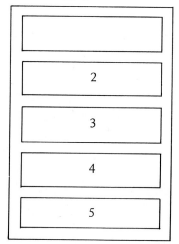

Colour Plate 5

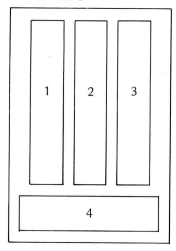

Colour Plate 6

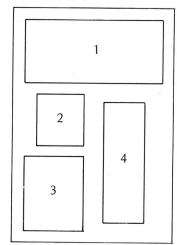

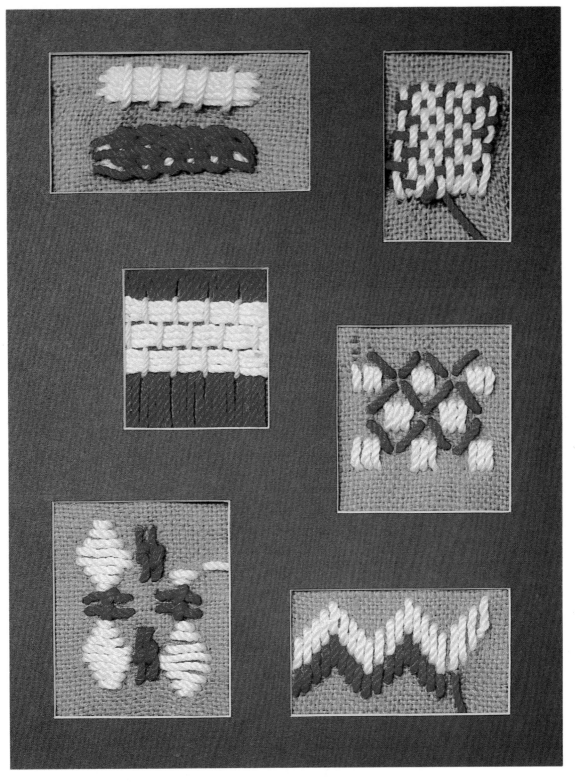

Plate 1

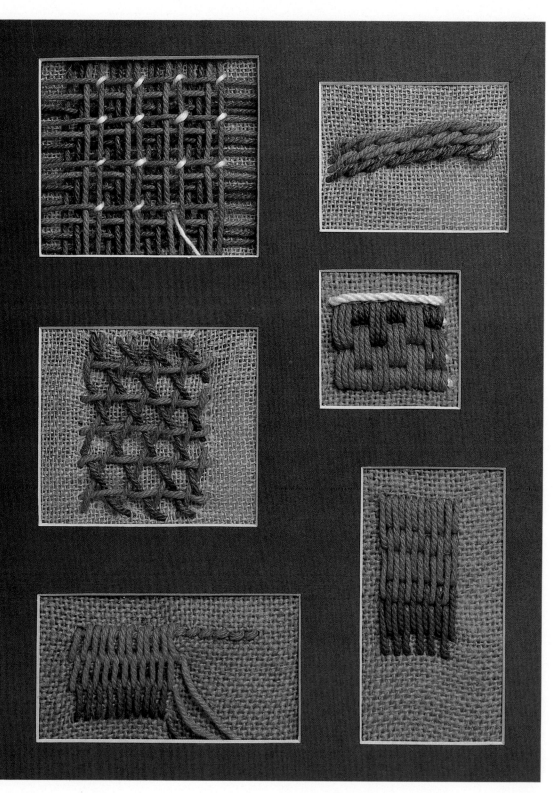

Plate 2

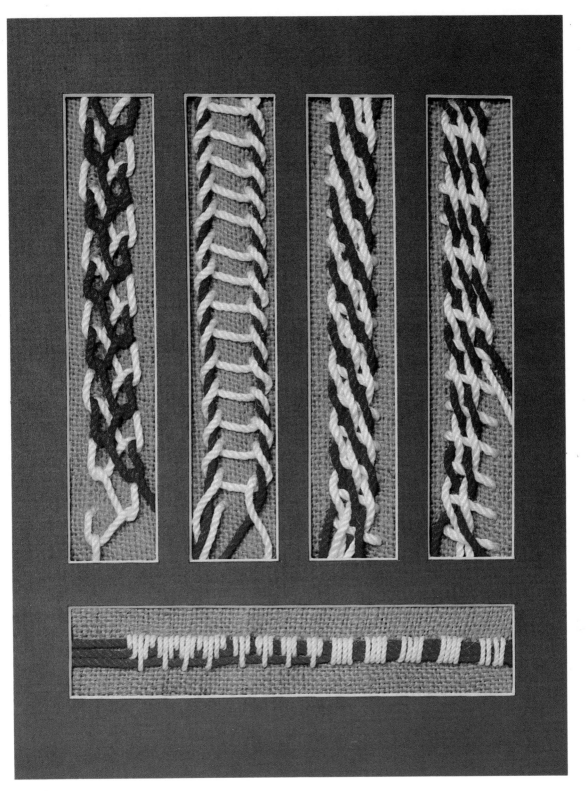

Plate 3

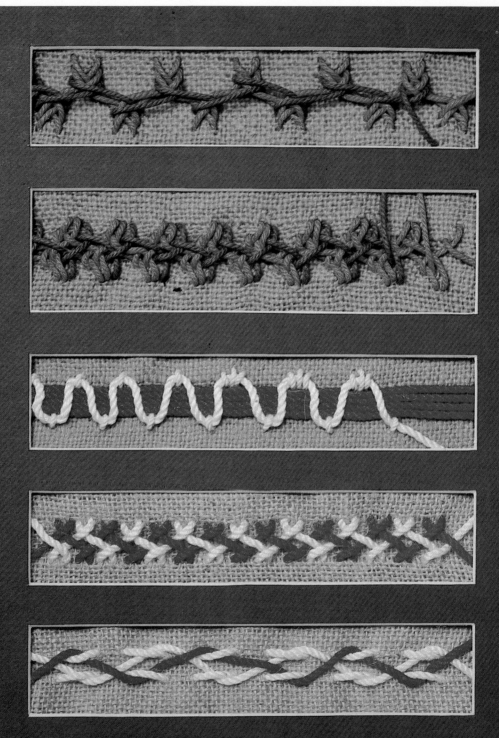

Plate 4

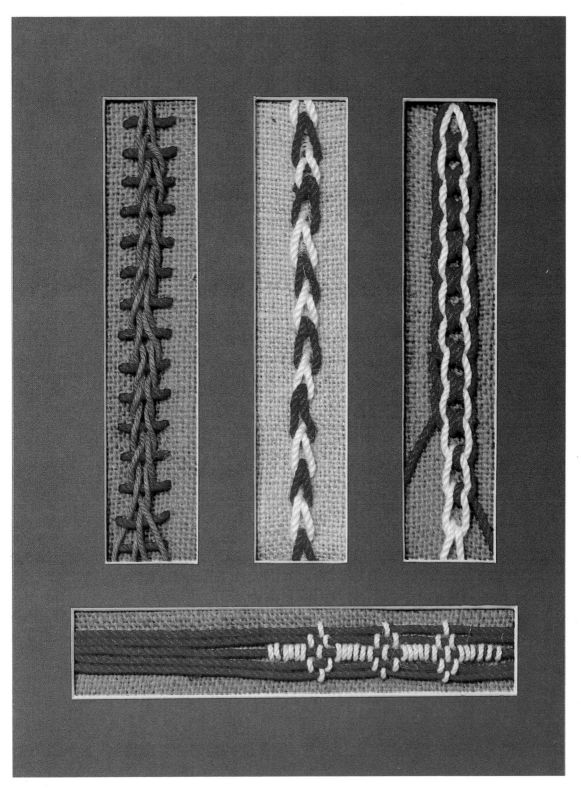

Plate 5

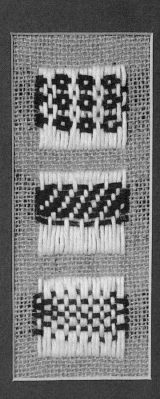

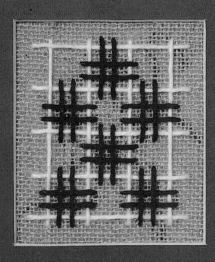

Plate 6

Raised buttonhole stitch on a raised band

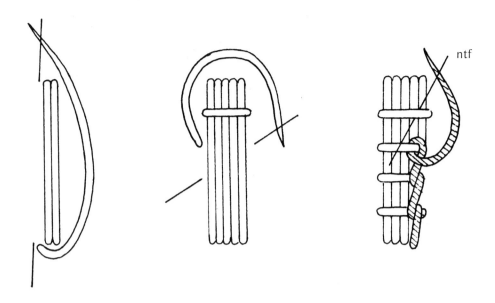

Surface and patterned darning

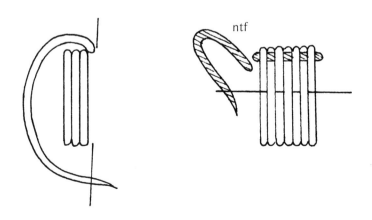

Raised couched filling basket stitch

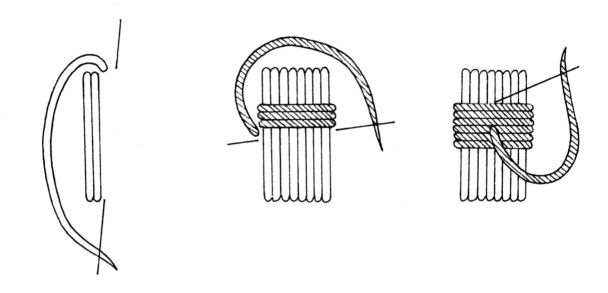

Squares and bundles

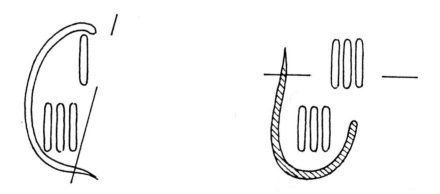

Diamond oriental filling

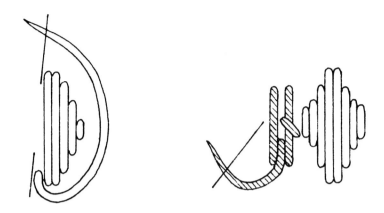

Satin stitch chevron filling

Battlement couching

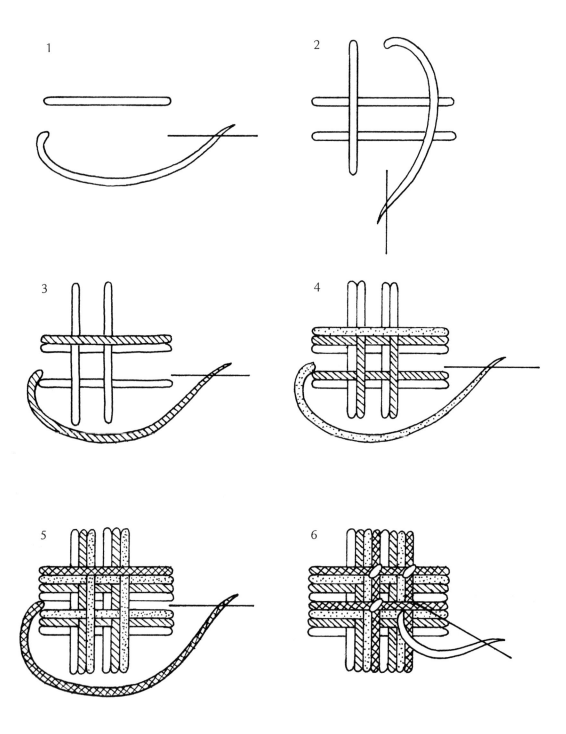

1

2

3

4

5

6

Shaded stem stitch filling

Honeycomb filling stitch

ntf

Chevron filling

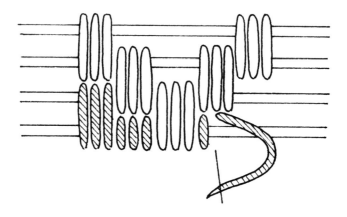

Block shading

Base of back stitch or split stitch

 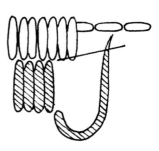

Long and short shading stitch

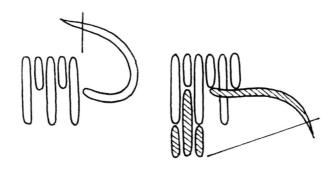

Plaited feather stitch

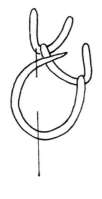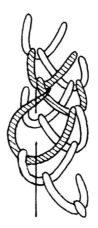

Singalese chain stitch

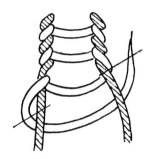

Diagonal woven band

Two needles are used to make this stitch
Start row with alternate colour

base

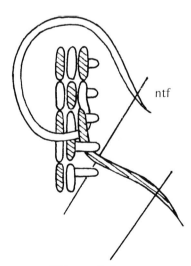

ntf

This needle hanging free

Striped woven band

Two needles are used to make this stitch
Start row with same colour

base

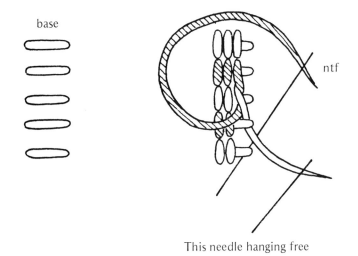

ntf

This needle hanging free

Patterned couching

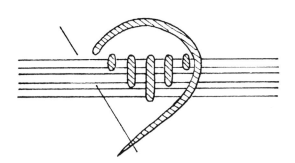

Triple herringbone stitch

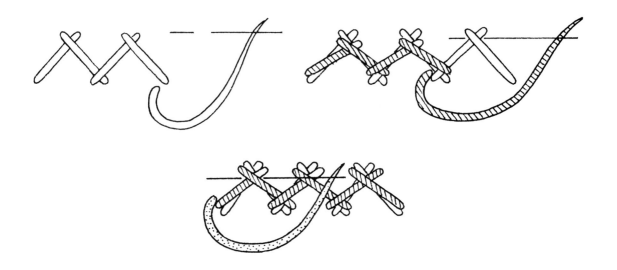

Triple cretan stitch

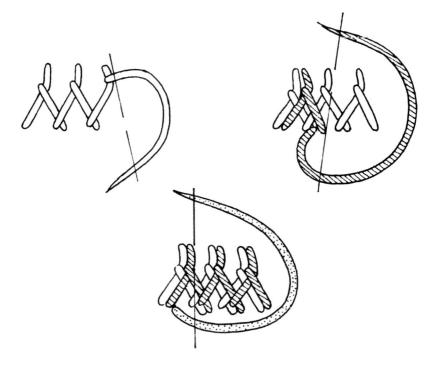

Persian border couching stitch

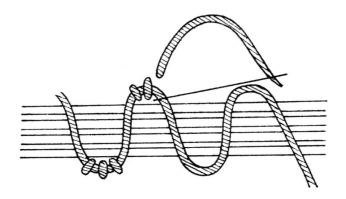

Double herringbone stitch

Actions as for an ordinary herringbone stitch, but often the needle is slipped under the thread

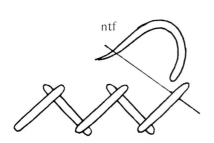

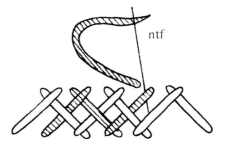

Laced double running stitch

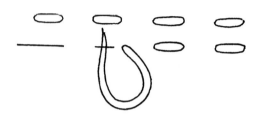

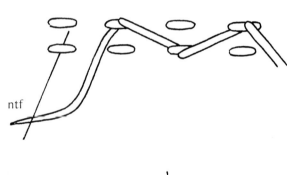

ntf

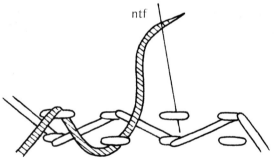

ntf

Checked chain band stitch

Two needles are used to make this stitch
Repeat 1 and 2 with needle b, alternate these stages with needles a and b

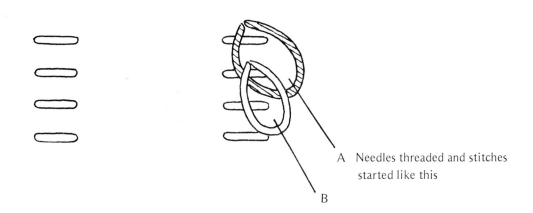

A   Needles threaded and stitches
    started like this

B

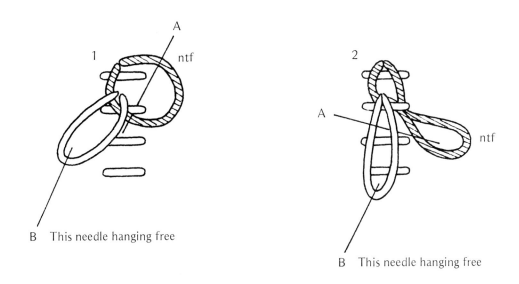

1   ntf

A

B   This needle hanging free

2

A

ntf

B   This needle hanging free

Chequered chain stitch

Needle threaded with two threads, each thread used alternately to make a chain

Interlaced chain stitch

Work this stitch down both sides of the chain stitch

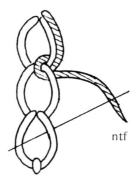

ntf

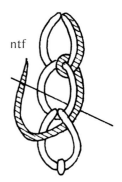

ntf

Fancy couching

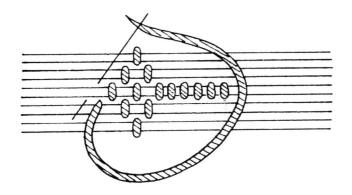

Darning huckaback
and fancy darning stitch

Threaded stitches worked on a huckaback fabric
The patterns are produced by the thread not going through the fabric
but by slipping under the float in this fabric
If the float is picked up at various intervals different patterns are produced

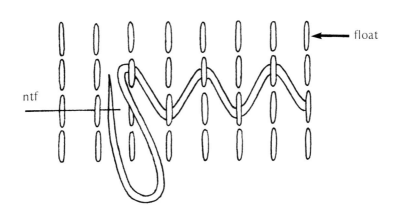

Plaid filling stitch

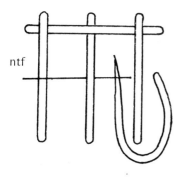

ntf

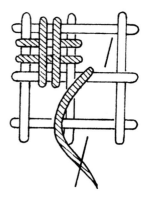

Patterned darning weaving

Different patterns are achieved on the base threads by
taking the top thread under the base threads, ntf, at various intervals

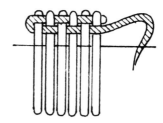

INDEX

Figures *in italics* refer to stitches which are also illustrated in the plates